THE PILLAR
OF THE WORLD

ANTONY AND CLEOPATRA
IN SHAKESPEARE'S
DEVELOPMENT

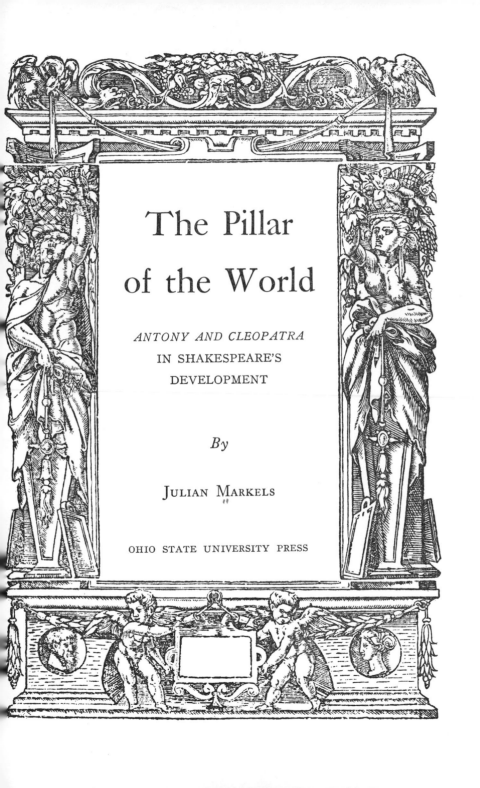

The Pillar
of the World

ANTONY AND CLEOPATRA
IN SHAKESPEARE'S
DEVELOPMENT

By

JULIAN MARKELS

OHIO STATE UNIVERSITY PRESS

For my mother,
FRIEDA MARKELS

Acknowledgments

IN ITS PROTRACTED GESTATION THIS BOOK HAS BENEFITED BY my conversations with many colleagues, friends, and relatives, especially William J. Brandt, Jules Chametzky, Donald R. Howard, Roberta Markels, and Harold R. Walley. My greatest debts are to my teacher Leonard Unger, who provided the example of his own criticism and who shared his thought with me while directing the studies from which the book has taken shape; and to my colleagues Richard D. Altick, Robert M. Estrich, and my wife Joan Webber, who read the several versions of the manuscript with a rigor that saved me from much error, and a responsiveness that taught me new facets of my argument. The book's remaining deficiencies are, of course, entirely my responsibility.

Contents

THE PILLAR
OF THE WORLD

ANTONY AND CLEOPATRA

IN SHAKESPEARE'S

DEVELOPMENT

ANTONY AND CLEOPATRA
IN SHAKESPEARE'S DEVELOPMENT

S HAKESPEARE, in a daring episode near the end of *Antony and Cleopatra,* turns you back on yourself and for a moment leaves you all alone. By now many awesome things have happened: fortunes have flowed with the moon, treaties and marriages have been made and broken, battles dared and deserted and won. Antony is dead, and Cleopatra has bargained with Caesar in her tomb. She knows now that if she lives she will be led through Rome in triumph, and she is preparing herself to die. Within a few lines the old man will bring at her request the asps whose biting, he says, is immortal. Now in her climactic motion, up toward the verge of death but with so much life still in her, Cleopatra looks back, imagining for a moment her appearance in Rome as an ornament to Caesar's triumph:

> Nay, 'tis most certain, Iras. Saucy lictors
> Will catch at us like strumpets, and scald rhymers
> Ballad us out o' tune. The quick comedians
> Extemporally will stage us and present
> Our Alexandrian revels. Antony
> Shall be brought drunken forth, and I shall see
> Some squeaking Cleopatra boy my greatness
> I' th' posture of a whore. (V.ii.214-21)

These lines are written for a boy actor who for two hours' traffic in the street of quick comedians has been squeaking out his Cleopatra in the posture of a whore. We might pass off the speech as a joke on him, to be relished by groundlings and courtiers alike, or we might quickly classify it as a conventional play upon the theme of appearance and reality. But these are inadequate responses to the fact revealed by the speech: that the performance on the stage and the reality it claims to imitate, though distinct from each other in all their concrete actualities, together create a unified experience that occurs outside of time. Suddenly this speech jolts us into the play as active participants in its artifice: we are made to change places with the playwright, even to defend his art against his assumed disbelief. We are briefly lifted out of ourselves and left to stand in his place; and just at this moment the creative insight asked of us is to imagine the historical Cleopatra and the boy actor as literal contemporaries, with all their differences intact, and yet all the distance between them erased. Imagining them in this way gives in turn a precise justification to Cleopatra's statement fifty lines later, as she robes herself for the asp, "I have/ Immortal longings in me." By holding poised in our minds the Queen of Egypt and her boy impersonator, in fact we create and experience the immortality of Cleopatra.[1]

I do not mean that Cleopatra's speech may be taken for the whole play, as a microcosm or focus for its major themes. Among great works of art only the whole may represent the whole. In fact this speech barely alludes to the important actions and ideas of *Antony and Cleopatra*. It does not condense or moralize our experience of the play by telling us, for example, that ripeness is all, or that we are such stuff as dreams are made on. Rather, the speech arrests for a moment our ongoing experience of the play in its unabbreviated wholeness. By subverting our suspension of disbelief and reminding us that we have been attending to a dream after all, it quickens our perception of the whole extent of the play as an emotional and intellectual experience, so that we may put a boundary around it in our minds and locate alongside the dream of the play the stuff of life outside it—the life of the actual Cleopatra wrinkled deep in time, and the flattened, squeaky presence of the boy actor. We are made aware of the world and the play at once, of the real Cleopatra and the postured one, not so that we may know how one is based on the other or how both are fused in a unique synthesis, but rather that we may see how each is a condition for the other, and both are simultaneous yet wholly distinct.

This experience comes only from an intense effort of imagination, which cannot be sustained for long. The experience of course is different from any description of it; but it is also very different from what our common notions of the subject lead us to expect. When we speak ordinarily of immortality, we are likely to think of some heroic deed or work of art passed down from hand to hand through generations, so that it is never past but always timely. But in the experience created by Cleopatra's speech, the spectator casts his mind back in time to perceive the past in its integrity without leaving the present, and by linking in awareness both past and present, to make them coexistent. This is an exercise of the historical imagination, in that it depends upon our ability to conceive the past in its separateness rather than upon the ability of the past to keep up to date. Neither Cleopatra's immortality nor that of Shakespeare is a device of their making, to be lifted and passed on to us like an eternal light. Rather, Cleopatra's immortality is a particular accomplishment of Shakespeare's historical imagination working through such episodes; and Shakespeare's immortality lies only with the power of our historical imagination to rekindle continuously.

These remarks are, of course, relevant to other plays, and to many things besides plays. Shakespeare's imagination has ensured the immortality of several historical figures besides Cleopatra, and in this he is not unique among the writers of the world. Nor is this speech the only place in Shakespeare or in world drama where the playwright conspicuously reminds us of our mutual make-believe. But the speech and the response it arouses are intrinsic to *Antony and Cleopatra,* and important for Shakespeare's meaning, in a unique way reflected by the arrest of attention commonly produced among sympathetic listeners by Cleopatra's words. Among other respects in which *Antony and Cleopatra* is distinctive among Shakespeare's plays is that here immortality is given thematic status as part of the play's subject. Hamlet at his death asks Horatio to tell the world his story, and Othello tries to ensure that his story will be transmitted accurately to posterity. But Mark Antony imagines a future with Cleopatra "Where souls do couch on flowers"; and Cleopatra, whom we were told age cannot wither, confirms Antony's expectations when she says, "I have/ Immortal longings in me," as if these were as concrete, as precisely located, and as easily satisfied as hunger pangs. In the context of the play this is not wishful thinking, and it is not a histrionic statement. As I will attempt to show later, her consummated experience in the play has schooled Cleopatra to her expectations by making her familiar with immortality.

In fact, the exercise of imagination invited by Cleopatra's speech is what finally makes us aware of the play's intellectual range and significance. It is no coincidence that in the very words by which Cleopatra and the boy actor become coexistent to our minds, so too do opposite judgments of Cleopatra:

> I shall see
> Some squeaking Cleopatra boy my greatness
> I' th' posture of a whore.

"Greatness" and "whore" both are accurate words for Cleopatra. But they do not cancel each other's meaning, and they do not fuse in a third meaning. Rather, each exerts its meaning inseparably from that of the other, and together they make a single imaginative perception. Cleopatra speaks as if greatness were her most certain and familiar attribute, and her concern over the accuracy with which she will be impersonated is surprising because Shakespeare has until now gone out of his way to portray her in the posture of a whore. In the first half of the play Shakespeare altered the Cleopatra he found in Plutarch by elaborating upon her seductiveness and decadence, and by suppressing all evidence of her culture and refinement. Plutarch said through North that Cleopatra was offended by Antony's coarse jests; that beauty was not her main attraction for men, but that "so sweete was her companie and conversacion, that a man could not possiblie but be taken"; that she had, in the Renaissance meaning of the term, a "curteous nature"; that her tongue was "an instrument of musicke" that had mastered the languages of almost every people with whom Egypt had diplomatic relations. Though disapprovingly aware of her qualities and accomplishments as a courtesan, Plutarch, by recording at the beginning these signs of her greatness, gave Cleopatra her regrettable due.[2] But Shakespeare will have none of them. In the first half of his play Cleopatra is alternately a wily temptress and a spitfire, vying with Antony at coarse jests, using her tongue as a scourge, and consistently exhibiting everything except a "curteous nature."

No doubt there is a certain playful virtuosity in Shakespeare's impulse to debase Cleopatra at first and then have her speak blithely of her greatness. Evoking her greatness by calling her a whore is as deft a stroke as invoking her presence by naming the boy actor. But this kind of virtuosity must rely on a genuine possibility of belief, and it is more than playful to suppose that "greatness" may be commensurate with "whore." By her style and finesse, Cleopatra surely raises whoring up to greatness, in the Aristotelian sense that every kind has its own excellence. But the lasting greatness for which we honor her is that she goes on to perform just the action one would least expect from a whore. She remains faithful to her lover after he dies, and in the act of affirming her greatness decides to kill herself in order to be reunited with him. "Husband, I come!" she says to Antony as she prepares for the asp; and the nobility of her act impresses us by the sharp contrast between her constancy now and her old fickleness. In Antony's "curteous" wife Octavia this sort of loyalty is not remarkable. But we are struck with wonder to see Cleopatra's Egyptian variety now subject to Roman discipline. The deepest meaning of her greatness is that she has been in the posture of a whore.

The adverse judgment implied by "whore" is transmuted when we confront the greatness whose meaning "whore" has made. By holding poised in our minds two morally contradictory actions, we transform all moral action into postures, which become not false poses but the protean forms of life. Step by step through this play Shakespeare has made us amoral, in order to produce at last an imaginative experience of omniscience to accompany the experience of timelessness. At this stage of his development amorality has nothing to do with the cynical Machiavellianism of his notorious villains, Richard III, Iago, and Edmund. It does not unleash evil upon the world, but releases good from evil like an athlete from the stone, and bears enigmatic witness to the two poised against each other. There are no villains in *Antony and Cleopatra,* not even such puny mischief-makers as the tribunes in *Julius Caesar.* Evil in that form had proved in *King Lear* to be self-destructive, and Shakespeare is no longer concerned with it directly. Here the evil to be conquered is not only within the characters themselves; it is the other side of their goodness. It is into mere whore and only into whore that the unique greatness of Cleopatra is in danger of falling. In the amoral vision I speak of, the whore in her is truly won over to its particular, inimitable greatness. What we call evil is assimilated in the all but mystical knowledge that the moral life is forever open to a breathtaking moment when such opposed qualities may become true conditions for each other, or when Mark Antony may become simultaneously "plated Mars" and "strumpet's fool," "husband" and "fire and air." Lear acquired this knowledge when, the evil of his world having proved self-destructive and his personal trials having won him to his greatness, he felt prepared at last to join Cordelia and "take upon's the mystery of things,/ As if we were God's spies." I believe that we must accept and share this knowledge if we are to have the meaning of *Antony and Cleopatra,* which seems to me nothing less than Shakespeare's attempt to elaborate and confirm the insight to which he had brought his protagonist and himself at the end of *King Lear.*

II

The play is built upon the opposition of public and private values.[3] However we name them—love or honour, lust or empire—we know from the moment of Philo's opening speech that the issue before us is the form in which this opposition is to be resolved. It is usually said that Mark Antony is confronted by a choice between the values represented by Cleopatra and those represented by Octavius Caesar; and that however inadequate either value might be, he resolves this conflict by choosing Cleopatra and giving up the world. Instead I shall argue in this book that Mark Antony is disciplined in the distinctive vision of the play, wherein he is challenged either to choose between the opposed values represented by Cleopatra and Octavius or not to choose between them; and that instead of choosing, he resolves the conflict by striving equally toward both values and rhythmically making each one a measure and condition of the other. The result of his effort is that instead of becoming more "effeminate," as in North's Plutarch, Shakespeare's Antony grows larger in manhood until he can encompass both Rome and Egypt, affirming the values that both have taught him until both are fulfilled. Then his death comes, as Cleopatra's does later, not as dissolution but as transcendence, a sign of his having approached as close to immortality as a poet may dare to imagine by becoming everything that it was in him to be. That I think is why the lovers' deaths produce a feeling of exaltation that so many critics find unique in Shakespeare. In the concrete detail of the play's rendition, these deaths are not permitted to break the continuity of existence. Antony kills himself with his own world-sharing sword, yet does not complete the work, so that he may be left to die upon a kiss, which in turn is not quite so much to die as to "melt" and "discandy." [4] Cleopatra desires death, like a "lover's pinch," to satisfy her immortal longing. She has found a means of death that will cause neither inward pain nor outward disfigurement; and she succeeds so well that in the embrace of the asp she merely "looks like sleep." For her and Antony death is not a limitation but a transformation of existence into a state of peace where the energy and the sweetness of life are at last unfettered. Their deaths signify not that one half of life is well lost for another but that both halves are found at last and hinged upon each other, in order that the whole world may be won.

This powerful element of transcendence in the death of the lovers, grounded as it is in their effort to reconcile public and private values by refusing to choose between them, marks an important stage in Shakespeare's development, and perhaps cannot begin to be understood outside the context of the Shakespearean canon. For one thing, the special poise in Shakespeare's treatment of death in this play suggests a familiar continuum. On the one hand, Antony and Cleopatra actually die, like the protagonists of the great tragedies, their physical deaths constituting a measure of providential judgment for their fully revealed human frailty. On the other hand, the tone of apotheosis in which their deaths are invested is in the symbolic key of Shakespeare's last plays, where death is no longer conceived naturalistically within the framework of a providential order, as in the tragedies, and is therefore no longer functional in the drama. Here as elsewhere *Antony and Cleopatra* goes far to bridge the difference between Shakespearean tragedy and romance.

Shakespeare's treatment of death in this play, moreover, is not simply a virtuoso performance isolated from the remainder of his concerns. There is a connection between the way the lovers die and the way they have lived, and their rewarding effort to reconcile public and private values locates *Antony and Cleopatra* on the central line of Shakespeare's development, where he is markedly concerned with this conflict of values in his history plays and Roman plays, in *Hamlet* and *King Lear* especially among the tragedies, and finally in *The Winter's Tale* and *The Tempest*. About this aspect of the play as well, it will be useful here to make a preliminary sketch of the argument to be developed in the following pages. Shakespeare's mind was formed in a community that felt itself to be achieving a precarious cultural and political unity after a devastating period of internal strife, and it was natural that early in his career Shakespeare, like many of his countrymen, should focus his attention on the two related problems of order in the state, and of the king's vocation in upholding that order. He began with a firm commitment to the doctrine that temporal order and the king's role are integrally related because both are divinely sanctioned and oriented.[5] But as he applied this doctrine to the presumed facts of history given him by his culture and to the facts of human nature discovered by his art, he came to question the divine self-regulating efficacy of a world order that had shown itself capable of such extensive breakdown as to provide him with the subject matter of his history plays. Simply the writing of such chronicle plays as Shakespeare's *Henry VI* and *Henry IV* cycles, instead of traditional morality plays or epics, served in fact to secularize the idea of world order, and to acknowledge politics as a fallen human activity rather than a divine sacrament. It is true that the chronicle plays typically attempt to picture the vicissitudes of politics as the temporal reflection of a providential scheme. But their subject is disorder in the human community, and first of all they are called upon to dramatize the human causes and consequences of disorder. The more coherent and effective they were to become as plays, the more vividly they had to reveal the personal character of the king, both in weakness and in strength, as the best available warrant for order in the kingdom. As this process of aesthetic growth took place, as the chronicle plays sharpened and refined their concern for the relationship between personal character and public order, they began implicitly to conceive the state not allegorically, as a work of God, but dramatically, as a work of art. The England of Shakespeare's history plays depends for her health and destiny upon the specifically human talents, the shaping imagination of her Richards and her Henrys. These men may claim divine stewardship for themselves, and others may claim it for them; but the program of the plays is to show how they use their human power, for better or for worse, to mold their country's character by making her history.

When the state becomes a work of art, so does the person; and one of the striking elements in Shakespeare's history plays is the self-consciousness with which he invests his heroes. A passage from Burckhardt's *The Civilization of the Renaissance in Italy* will suggest the background for this phenomenon:

> In the Middle Ages both sides of human consciousness—that which was turned within and that which was turned without—lay as though dreaming or half awake beneath a common veil. . . . Man was conscious of himself only as a member of a race, people, party, family, or corporation—only through some general category. It is in Italy that this veil dissolved first; there arose an *objective* treatment and consideration of the State and of all the things of this world, and at the same time the *subjective* side asserted itself with corresponding emphasis. Man became a spiritual *individual,* and recognized himself as such.[6]

Burckhardt is speaking of developments in Italy during the fourteenth and fifteenth centuries, and his remarks are relevant to Shakespeare's treatment of British history during the same period. It is a commonplace that in Shakespeare's history plays from *Richard II* to *Henry V* we see many facets of the transition from a medieval to a modern conception of national politics and public life, especially in the career of Prince Hal. Henry Bolingbroke and his son Hal, in contrast to Richard II and Hotspur, respectively, begin to conceive the state as an object of deliberate policy instead of ritual passion. Their desire to undertake foreign campaigns in order to distract their subjects from domestic rivalries, and thereby to unite the nation behind them, typifies their sophisticated statecraft. With what the Elizabethans would have called a similarly Machiavellian adroitness, in their personal conduct they play shrewdly imagined roles in relation to their subjects, Prince Hal to such an extent that it is impossible to separate the man from the self-dramatized public image. In his opening soliloquy, in his several claims for the educational value of his tavern life, in his trying the crown for size and his prompt defense of this premature experiment, and in his strained attempt at democratic comradeship with the common soldiers in *Henry V,* Hal is continuously stage-managing his effects and theatrically improvising his character as he goes along. Whatever might be his exact proportion of histrionic calculation at any given moment, he is almost never free of that pagan impulse to shape himself in images that he announced in his opening soliloquy.

I shall have more to say later about the manifold detail of self-dramatization in Prince Hal and other Shakespearean heroes. Here I suggest only that for Shakespeare as he matures, the political leader's impulse toward self-dramatization becomes problematical, along with political order itself, as inseparable parts of a single awareness. The earlier concern for the perma nence of order is progressively subordinated to a concern for that discrepancy between public and private values that *Antony and Cleopatra* is to call by the names of Rome and Egypt. In the history plays it is clear that the king's vocation, in order to deserve its divine sanction, requires the subordination of private values to that "ceremony" of the public world that King Henry V explains in a notable speech of regret after he has purged himself, as Prince Hal, both of his earlier image of himself and of Falstaff. In fact, the friction between character and "ceremony" underlies the protagonist's self-dramatization as he tries to satisfy the public demands made upon him. This personal conflict between private and public loyalties influences in turn the ongoing politics of order, to complete a vicious circle: Shakespeare comes to recognize that the protagonist's histrionics may themselves constitute an original public fact, a cause rather than a symptom of political instability. This perception, fundamental to *Richard II,* is explored and enlarged in *Julius Caesar, Hamlet,* and *King Lear,* among the plays to be discussed in this book. In these plays political ethics, and especially the psychological basis for ethics, become as important as the structure of public order. The private lives of Richard, Brutus, Hamlet, and Lear are threatened by self-dramatization no less regularly, and no less independently, than their political communities are subject to the vicissitudes of rebellion, usurpation, and anarchy. Character and society keep failing each other more and more, until the circle is broken in *King Lear.* There the self-dramatization of an aging king begins the dissolution of public order; once under way, the public disorder intensifies the private; and the fearful point is reached where each must complete itself separately, at the edge of doom, before public and private life both can be reconstituted. In *King Lear* public and private values, and beyond those values good and evil themselves, no longer are conceived in causal relations with each other; all virtues and flaws have become original and autonomous. If we can speak at all of divine providence in *King Lear*, we cannot say that it guarantees the continuity of political order, but only that it underwrites the existence of Cordelia as well as Edmund, so that life may continue if man chooses. Order and disorder, both public and private, are shown to be ineradicable potentialities of life; and personal self-dramatization is separated from politics and made an independent problem of vocation.

So much of Shakespeare's career falls into place in *King Lear*, and *King Lear* is so great a play in its own right, that it is difficult not to conclude that Shakespeare's development ends and culminates there. But this view impoverishes Shakespeare, whose development does not culminate anywhere but goes on through *Antony and Cleopatra* and other plays, to end where he ends, with *The Tempest*. In that development *Antony and Cleopatra* goes beyond *King Lear*—not above it but beyond it, to break new ground, and to fill out the whole contour of Shakespeare's development. The opposite of self-dramatization, Regan herself tells us in *King Lear*, is self-knowledge. By the time Lear achieves what measure of self-knowledge he is granted, he wants the safety of a "wall'd prison" to protect his personal accomplishment from any further threat of public life. One reason he is denied even this rescue is that Shakespeare has come to see that self-knowledge is not a condition but a process, like life itself, in which public and private values must remain in continuing negotiation with each other and in which not even the old and wise are permitted a separate peace, as Prospero will come to recognize. Meanwhile Shakespeare creates in Antony a character whose earned self-knowledge does not result in a desire to renounce the world for the safety of Lear's prison, but instead a desire to remain in the world, and, since it must continue to suffer his flaws, a magnanimous insistence upon giving freely to his world of his strength, virtue, and treasure as well. By accepting fully his own imperfection along with the world's, Antony is able to remain unprotected, and to let what goodness he has earned perform whatever acts of magnanimity are possible. For Shakespeare in *Antony and Cleopatra,* then, self-knowledge and the virtue it entails become not a place but a pathway, continually renewed in and through public action; and Shakespeare's progression from *King Lear* to *Antony and Cleopatra* is toward this conception, with its corollary vision of the immortal joining of public and private values.

CHAPTER TWO

THE PUBLIC AND PRIVATE WORLDS
OF *ANTONY AND CLEOPATRA*

A NTONY's Roman duty and his Egyptian appetite are represented as necessary alternatives in the beginning. Though Cleopatra is to be regarded neither as the object of a Wagnerian passion nor as a passing itch, she is placed clearly at the center of Antony's private life, which everywhere in the first act is weighed against his public commitments. Philo, Antony's friend, names the conflict in the opening speech of the play:

> His captain's heart,
> Which in the scuffles of great fights hath burst
> The buckles on his breast, reneges all temper
> And is become the bellows and the fan
> To cool a gypsy's lust. (I.i.6–10)

Octavius, Antony's arch competitor, echoes this when he complains that while Pompey threatens immediate danger to the state, Antony "fishes, drinks, and wastes/ The lamps of night in revel." And Pompey hopes that Cleopatra will continue to "Tie up the libertine in a field of feasts." However they may scramble among themselves to rule the world, all Romans are of one mind concerning the lapse of Antony in his relation with Cleopatra.

Cleopatra herself is really of their mind. Though later in the play Antony's death will teach her otherwise, now she agrees that he cannot hold up his head both in Rome and Egypt at once. She also would have him choose. But, of course, she does not share the Roman estimate of Egypt or herself; and she uses all her wiles to intensify Antony's awareness of the conflict and to make him choose her. She taunts him endlessly for all his Roman ties of loyalty and duty. When Antony refuses to hear the messengers from Rome, she teases him to give them audience and thus show his subservience to "the scarce-bearded Caesar." When he names his boundless love for her as a reason for ignoring the messengers, she asks why then is he married to Fulvia. When later he reassures her that Fulvia is dead, she pretends to discover in his cool response to Fulvia's death a forecast of his indifference to hers. She damns him if he loves Fulvia, and also if he doesn't. In crossing him at every turn, she is pursuing that feminine strategy which she thinks will best sustain his love; and her strategy assumes that Rome and Egypt are irreconcilable alternatives. Later in the play the strategy will prove ineffectual because its underlying assumption is inaccurate. But here it indicates the pervasiveness of that assumption early in the play.

Both the Roman leaders and Cleopatra, then, identify unmistakably the conflict of values that faces Antony. But Antony himself lives the conflict; in him it is internal. He begins by sharing the general opinion that he must choose between Rome and Egypt and by rejecting one for the other. At first he wants only "some pleasure now," and will not hear the news from Rome. Later, having heard the messengers, he decides he must break with Cleopatra "Or lose myself in dotage." Nothing shows better how deeply he is divided than the sharp contrast in style between the speech in which he refuses audience to the Roman messengers and the speech in which he later announces to Cleopatra his departure for Rome. I place the two speeches consecutively in order to dramatize the contrast.

> Let Rome in Tiber melt and the wide arch
> Of the rang'd empire fall! Here is my space.
> Kingdoms are clay; our dungy earth alike
> Feeds beast as man. The nobleness of life
> Is to do thus [*embracing*] ; when such a mutual pair
> And such a twain can do't, in which I bind,
> On pain of punishment, the world to weet
> We stand up peerless. (I.i.33–40)

>   Hear me, Queen.
> The strong necessity of time commands
> Our services awhile; but my full heart
> Remains in use with you. Our Italy
> Shines o'er with civil swords. Sextus Pompeius
> Makes his approaches to the port of Rome.
> Equality of two domestic powers
> Breeds scrupulous faction. The hated, grown to strength,
> Are newly grown to love. The condemn'd Pompey,
> Rich in his father's honour, creeps apace
> Into the hearts of such as have not thriv'd
> Upon the present state, whose numbers threaten;
> And quietness, grown sick of rest, would purge
> By any desperate change. My more particular,
> And that which most with you should safe my going,
> Is Fulvia's death. (I.iii.41–56)

A stranger could not easily guess that both these speeches are by Antony. The first is personal and passionate, breathless with the lover's intensity. Its words spill over into gestures, as Antony embraces Cleopatra when he says, "the nobleness of life/ Is to do thus." The diction is concrete, the imagery vivid and vast. It has already that Brobdingnagian quality[1] characteristic of the whole play, in which language strains its limits in order to encompass its subject. And the syntax is simple, swift, and compact, with those quick transitions and elisions of thought that attempt to embody Antony's passion even as they dilate it.

In contrast to the assurance and intensity of this opening speech and his action following it, there is a defensive, measured tone in the second speech and everything relating to Antony's departure from Egypt. He has tried five times during the conversation to explain his purpose, and each time Cleopatra has interrupted and distracted him. Now at last he bursts out in a highly wrought forensic style, verbose instead of breathless: the passionless impersonal style of the public Roman. His diction this time is abstract and his imagery is generalized. His measured rhythm struts with dignity; and his syntax is carefully articulated, replete with subordination, as if to support by sentence structure that wide arch of the ranged empire that he was ready to let fall before.

The contrast between the speeches shows Antony caught between two values. I think it even hints at the incompleteness of one value without the other, for each speech in its own way is rhetorically overdone, as if to justify by the incantation of a style what cannot be defended by reason: Antony's alarming indifference to the condition of Rome on the one hand, and on the other his frightening neglect of his full heart's desire. In any case, believing with the others that a choice is required, Antony chooses Rome, and thus initiates a process whereby he is to master the Roman public world and encompass its values. Before following that process in detail, however, we must see in what respects the presentation of Antony in these opening scenes is symptomatic of the whole play. The contrast between the two speeches reveals Antony's temperament, and shows the particular form in which he is to suffer his trial and his ecstasy. Antony is not in the condition that post-Freudian thought calls "conflicted." He is not aware all at once of contradictory alternatives, then torn and weakened by the need to decide, and finally rendered impotent or else aloof, and in either case unready for action. Antony's way is precisely not to weigh his alternatives and divide himself against himself, but to live each alternative in turn, and lift his whole self back and forth across the line that divides Rome from Egypt. He devotes himself wholly to each world in turn, at first dismissing the Roman messengers with "There's not a minute of our lives should stretch/ Without some pleasure now"; and later dismissing himself from Egypt with "The strong necessity of time commands/ Our services awhile." He lives for the moment, indeed; but he is to give himself just as fully to the Roman moment as to the Egyptian. In each place where he stands is obliterated every connection with another time, place, or value. This discontinuity in thought and action is distinctive of Antony's character, and it is pervasive in the play, where character and conduct, motive and action, cause and effect, are everywhere forced apart and hidden from each other. On this score our perplexity only begins with Antony's two speeches, which generate in turn a whole series of questions. When did he

change his mind and decide to hear the messengers after all?
Why did he change his mind? And having heard the messengers,
why did he decide to leave Cleopatra and return to Rome?
Here it may seem obvious from the news the messengers have
brought him that his presence in Rome is required immediately.
But to Philo and Cleopatra that was obvious before the messengers had spoken. There were good reasons, they both knew,
why Antony should be in Rome—unless he were indeed willing
to see Rome fall. Our question is not whether the reasons he
finally enumerates are sufficient to justify Antony's departure
for Rome. Our question is rather when, where, how, and why
did Antony decide *not* to "Let Rome in Tiber melt"? And on
that question Antony, and behind him Shakespeare, is dazzlingly
silent. Antony's last words before his exit at I.i.55 are these
to the messengers: "Speak not to us." At his next entrance,
at I.ii.85, he is accompanied by a messenger who is in the
midst of giving him the news from Rome.

There are other striking reversals and discontinuities. When
he hears from the messenger that Fulvia is dead, Antony says,
" . . . she's good, being gone,/ The hand could pluck her back
that shov'd her on." And now that Fulvia is gone, just when we
might think that Antony is more free than ever to remain in
Egypt, he decides to return to Rome. His apparently impulsive
conduct is essentially like that which Cleopatra pursues as a
deliberate policy:

> See where he is, who's with him, what he does.
> I did not send you. If you find him sad,
> Say I am dancing; if in mirth, report
> That I am sudden sick. Quick, and return!
> (I.iii.2–5)

Nothing remains stable, predictable, "in character." Everywhere
we see reversal and change, and nowhere are we permitted even
to glimpse a reason for the change. Just as Antony weighs his
alternatives only by living them, so his every living action seems
uncaused, self-generated, a new creation whose spontaneity
disarms our challenge.

There is no reason to doubt that Shakespeare is perfectly in control of himself in these opening scenes, and hence that the discontinuities I have noted are precisely what he wants. We have no warrant for improving upon his alleged carelessness and ignoring the discontinuities by inventing for Antony a familiar rationale: that the Antony who speaks "Let Rome in Tiber melt" is a reeling infatuate, wined, dined, and whored out of his senses; whereas the Antony who speaks "The strong necessity of time commands/ Our services awhile" is back in his right mind and a proper man again. This customary interpretation furnishes Antony with a conventional psychology and his several actions with sufficient causes. But it goes straight against the grain of Shakespeare's portrait. Shakespeare gives us no warrant for believing that the wooden, lifeless style of Antony's second speech is "in character" and that the vital, passionate utterance of his first speech is not. And unlike Plutarch, he makes no claim that the action contemplated by one speech is preferable to that contemplated by the other. For Shakespeare both sides of Antony are in character, and each side is integral, discontinuous from the other. This early in the play we can only accept the discontinuity, see where Shakespeare will lead us with it, and let it become meaningful, if it can, in its own terms.

At crucial moments later in the play—for example, in his decisions to return from Rome to Egypt, to fight at Actium by sea, and to follow Cleopatra when she deserts that battle— Antony acts again without visible premeditation, in the same discontinuous manner as in the opening scenes. Such episodes will invite tampering and misinterpretation unless we have let ourselves be prepared by the opening scenes to see that all the discontinuities, instead of needing to be "resolved" and explained away, are intrinsic to Shakespeare's construction, are in fact the distinctive materials in the play's tight and luminous fabric. Then we might see too that Antony's conflict throughout is truly an internal one, though he does not deliberate his choices in full torment as Hamlet does, because so continuous an alternation in his whole style as a person necessarily involves a series of inner transformations. It is a characteristic and coherent response to experience and not an accidental or frivolous posture. His sudden and unexplained shifts throughout the play show the contour of Antony's mind, the quality of its anguish, and its continuing danger of being loosened from its moorings. Antony, like Lear, is not an introspective character; he is not divided up into direct discourse, soliloquy, and aside, so to speak, in order to give each part of his psyche its own distinct voice. He is just that man in whom there is no division between "inner" and "outer." But it does not follow that he is only a reprobate with no inner life at all. Although his inner life is less vivid and fractured than Hamlet's and Macbeth's, for example, I hope to show that it is equally intense; and I will argue later that it is no less humanly significant than theirs. Shakespeare's presentation of Antony in the opening scenes trains us in that awareness.

II

From the time Antony leaves Egypt, at the end of I.iii, until the time when his new wife Octavia leaves him at Athens, at the end of III.iv, Antony devotes himself to satisfying both in letter and in spirit his country's claim upon him. Back in Rome, confronted with the embarrassing fact that his wife Fulvia had made war upon his partner Caesar while he was fishing in the Nile, Antony begins by patching up his excuses to Caesar with whatever temporizing and self-deception are necessary. He argues that Fulvia's wars against Caesar were subtly directed against himself as well to get him away from Cleopatra, but that honor and good breeding required that he stay in Egypt and avoid meeting his own wife and brother in battle. Now he takes occasion to joke about Fulvia,

> As for my wife,
> I would you had her spirit in such another!
> The third o' th' world is yours, which with a snaffle
> You may pace easy, but not such a wife. (II.ii.61–64)

when a short time before, upon hearing of her death, he said how dear she was now that she was gone. This expedient change of attitude toward Fulvia is matched by an equally gross disloyalty to Cleopatra. Having pleaded first that honor made him stay there, soon Antony finds it convenient to regard his sojourn in Egypt as a lapse. To the charge that he has denied military aid to Caesar in those wars "Which fronted mine own peace," he replies:

> Neglected rather;
> And then when poisoned hours had bound me up
> From mine own knowledge. As nearly as I may,
> I'll play the penitent to you; but mine honesty
> Shall not make poor my greatness, nor my power
> Work without it. Truth is, that Fulvia,
> To have me out of Egypt, made wars here,
> For which myself, the ignorant motive, do
> So far ask pardon as befits mine honour
> To stoop in such a case. (II.ii.89–98)

The more he attempts to justify himself, the more desperately he fastens upon any argument that lies at hand, no matter how incoherent or debasing to his manhood. He ends by abandoning all pretense of argument, resorting to a compulsive assertion of his honor independently of anything he has done to maintain that honor. For as long as Antony is bent only upon making peace with Octavius and renewing his credentials in the Roman world, he has forfeited his only possible argument: that to him Egypt and Cleopatra represent indispensable human values. What Octavius has called his "lascivious wassails" Antony described earlier as "the nobleness of life." But now while Antony chooses to share Octavius' standards, his life in the East is wholly vulnerable to Octavius' criticism, and he is barred from making a plausible defense of his conduct.

Ironically, Antony's shabby rationalizations brilliantly serve their immediate purpose of restoring his pre-eminence in the Roman world, even to the point of making him an eligible husband for Octavia. The essential Roman issue is not Antony's past conduct but his political reliability in the future. Octavius,

who needs Antony's strength and skill in the expected war with
Pompey, is not eager to scruple nicely about honor at such a
moment. He wants from Antony a quick sign of good intentions,
some gesture of willingness that will justify him in binding his
sister in marriage to Antony. Thus Antony's empty posturing
is exquisitely matched by the ethical shallowness of Octavius'
response, for Octavius is willing to respect a mere show of
honor if it helps to consolidate his power.

But Antony does not continue merely to put on a show
until he can return conveniently to Egypt. The unimproved
flimsiness of his patched alliance with Octavius is not enough
at best to maintain his restored status among the Romans. Nor
can his large spirit have its measure taken by any form of
abject timeserving. Once turned back toward Rome, Antony
progresses from a mere posture to a committed pursuit of the
inner spirit of Roman honor. Immediately after his marriage,
he says:

> My Octavia,
> Read not my blemishes in the world's report.
> I have not kept my square; but that to come
> Shall all be done by th' rule. Good night, dear lady.
> (II.iii.4–7)

This candid statement is accurate both about his past and his
future. With Octavia he does not temporize as he did with her
brother. He makes no excuses for his past; and the sincerity
of his promise for the future is to be borne out by events.

Immediately after the speech quoted above, Octavia exits
and Antony's Egyptian soothsayer enters. Antony, palpably
satisfied by the progress of his affairs in Rome, asks the
soothsayer: "Now, sirrah; you do wish yourself in Egypt?"
The soothsayer wishes them both in Egypt, for, as he says,
though Antony is a better man than Caesar—"Noble, coura-
geous, high, unmatchable,"—Caesar has the better luck. Once
near Caesar, Antony's good angel leaves him, so that Caesar
invariably beats him against the odds. This reminder overturns
Antony's high spirits, and after the soothsayer exits, Antony

confesses that what he said is right. Then, less than forty lines after he has promised Octavia to live by the rule, Antony says:

> I will to Egypt;
> And though I make this marriage for my peace,
> I' th' East my pleasure lies. (II.iii.38–40)

These lines more than any other provide grounds for the customary interpretation of Antony's activity at Rome: that out of weakness or cynicism, no matter which, Antony is simply mending his political fences and watching hawk-eyed for the earliest opportunity to return to Egypt. There is a discontinuity indeed between Antony's promise to Octavia and his promise to himself; and this one surely lends color to the traditional view of Antony's dissolute character.

But here is just the moment when Antony stops vacillating between two worlds in Drydenesque fashion and begins to make each value, Rome and Egypt, relevant to the other. He means everything he says in both speeches, and neither one supersedes the other. What he calls his "pleasure" surely has its dissolute side; but it is neither dissolute nor contradictory to want to live by the rule and still to take pleasure in life. The soothsayer reminded him, after all, that he is overshadowed even in those pastimes that the austere Octavius allows himself; and it is a fair inference that his pain here lies in fully recognizing the circumscription of Roman values for the first time since his return. Antony's sudden depression of spirits after the soothsayer's speech suggests that his marriage to Octavia was neither desperate nor disingenuous. He took pleasure in his marriage, and his leading question to the soothsayer implies that he for one does *not* wish himself back in Egypt. When the soothsayer reminds him of his fainting luck in Caesar's presence, to be sure, he changes his mind with characteristic abruptness. But this time his newly aroused desire does not lead him to jump for Egypt at the first opportunity, or to break his promise to Octavia and stop living by the rule. Although he is still divided between Rome and Egypt, now for the first time he stops rejecting one for the other. In his remaining conduct throughout the play, the two values gradually become coexistent in his mind and conditional upon each other. Antony comes slowly to realize that he cannot escape Caesar's better luck, but still must put his virtue and his honor in the scales against it. He comes to recognize that the Roman peace upon which his Egyptian pleasure depends can be achieved only by the fact and not the show of honor; that his aspirations must sustain each other rather than compete. If there is little doubt in his mind or in ours that he will return to Egypt, the crucial fact is that he does not take the opportunity until he has fulfilled himself as a Roman, until he has lived conscientiously "by th' rule" and found himself betrayed in that conduct by lucky Caesar himself. Only when he discovers what he could not have anticipated, that Octavius rather than he has acted unconscionably, does Antony turn back toward Cleopatra. By then he has become the best of Romans, and even then he does not permit his conduct back in Egypt to undermine his reinstated Roman honor.

The immediate task of the reunited triumvirs is to settle their business with Pompey. Antony had wished to avoid war with Pompey, if he could also avoid debasing his reputation into the bargain:

> I did not think to draw my sword 'gainst Pompey;
> For he hath laid strange courtesies and great
> Of late upon me. I must thank him only,
> Lest my remembrance suffer ill report;
> At heel of that, defy him. (II.ii.156–60)

He had been unwilling to defy Octavius, and thus had lost his honor while protesting it. But now he takes the initiative in negotiating with Pompey an acceptable peace, which manifests simultaneously Antony's desire to avoid bloodshed, his uncertainty over the outcome of a possible battle, his personal regard for Pompey, and yet his readiness to defy Pompey and all these personal considerations for the sake of the public order at stake. Now for the first time we see him masterfully hinge together his public and private interests, and thereby displace Octavius in the seat of leadership. The episode needs to be quoted at length, in order to show both the ease with which Antony is here in command and the striking contrast between his assured deployment of his honor here and his stammering rationalizations in his earlier peacemaking with Octavius.

Ant. Thou canst not fear us, Pompey, with thy sails.
We'll speak with thee at sea. At land thou know'st
How much we do o'ercount thee.

Pom. At land indeed
Thou dost o'ercount me of my father's house!
But since the cuckoo builds not for himself,
Remain in't as thou mayst.

Lep. Be pleas'd to tell us
(For this is from the present) how you take
The offers we have sent you.

Caes. There's the point.

Ant. Which do not be entreated to, but weigh
What it is worth embrac'd.

Caes. And what may follow,
To try a larger fortune.

Pom. You have made me offer
Of Sicily, Sardinia; and I must
Rid all the sea of pirates; then, to send
Measures of wheat to Rome; this 'greed upon,
To part with unhack'd edges and bear back
Our targes undinted.

Omnes. That's our offer.

Pom. Know then
I came before you here a man prepar'd
To take this offer; but Mark Antony
Put me to some impatience. Though I lose
The praise of it by telling, you must know,
When Caesar and your brother were at blows,
Your mother came to Sicily and did find
Her welcome friendly.

Ant. I have heard it, Pompey,
And am well studied for a liberal thanks,
Which I do owe you.

Pom.   Let me have your hand.
          I did not think, sir, to have met you here.

Ant.   The beds i' th' East are soft; and thanks to you,
          That call'd me timelier than my purpose hither;
          For I have gain'd by't. (II.vi.24–53)

Here Lepidus plays his usual role of herald, while Octavius
merely seconds his colleagues with a polite form of browbeating.
To Antony falls the most delicate part of the negotiation,
especially in acquitting himself of Pompey's special grievance
against him. Antony refuses to threaten or to distort the facts
in order to gain a rhetorical advantage over Pompey, and in
the process he gains the desired advantage. He does not deny
Pompey's naval superiority; and whereas Octavius threatens
Pompey with the dangers of refusing their offer, Antony invites
him to consider the intrinsic value of that offer. Even his final
indirect reference to Cleopatra bears a new significance, through
which we see Rome and Egypt becoming simultaneous values
for him. To Octavius he had apologized for his "poisoned
hours" in Egypt and abased himself in the false confession
implied by that metaphor. To Octavia he had spoken broadly
of not having kept his square, but without embarrassing himself
by specific admissions. Now to Pompey he says only that the
beds in the East are soft, which sounds less like a confession of
guilt than an estimate of value. In suavely thanking Pompey
for taking him away from his soft bed, he begins to put his
Egyptian idyll beyond the reach of Roman criticism; and then
he turns discontinuously to the present and says he has gained
by his return to Rome.

What he has gained is Octavia; and the play goes on to
demonstrate the sincerity with which he values that gain. Caesar
has doubts, understandably; and long after Antony has said
that he makes this marriage only for his peace, Caesar presses
him on just that point at the time of their farewell:

Caes.   Most noble Antony,
          Let not the piece of virtue which is set

Betwixt us as the cement of our love
To keep it builded, be the ram to batter
The fortress of it; for better might we
Have lov'd without this mean, if on both parts
This be not cherish'd.

Ant.   Make me not offended
In your distrust.

Caes.   I have said.

Ant.   You shall not find,
Though you be therein curious, the least cause
For what you seem to fear. So the gods keep you
And make the hearts of Romans serve your ends!
We will here part. (III.ii.27–38)

When Octavius and Octavia exchange farewells, Antony says of his wife "The April's in her eyes. It is love's spring,/ And these the showers to bring it on. Be cheerful." The episode is highly complex. On the one hand, Shakespeare has gone out of his way, in an already crowded plot, to conduct this test of Antony's probity. But he offers no immediate evidence, either in the tone of Antony's speeches or in the surrounding context, that Antony is guilty of duplicity. On the contrary, Antony's beautiful description of Octavia, which continues throughout another speech beginning "Her tongue will not obey her heart" (III.ii.47–50), shows a true and eloquent lover. Yet we all heard Antony say before that he makes this marriage for his peace. If we confine our attention to this episode in context, then I do not see how we can believe that Antony's speech hides a deliberate intention to return to Egypt. If Antony is dissembling here, then his cynicism is even greater than his most severe detractors have claimed, and the play itself becomes an incoherent babble in which we cannot trust what the poetry tells us. Everything in Antony's utterance bespeaks the honor of his motives and the integrity of his love; and we can only conclude that if he said before that he makes this marriage for his peace, that is distinctly not what he is saying now. The two statements are simply discontinuous; and yet the action of the play does not permit either one to supersede the other.

Only in the light of the genuine honor won by his marriage to Octavia and his negotiation with Pompey may we discover the significance of Antony's departure for Egypt when it finally comes. In the scene of his farewell to Octavia, he begins by listing the grievances that have turned him against her brother:

> Nay, nay, Octavia; not only that—
> That were excusable, that and thousands more
> Of semblable import—but he hath wag'd
> New wars 'gainst Pompey; made his will, and read it
> To public ear;
> Spoke scantly of me: when perforce he could not
> But pay me terms of honour, cold and sickly
> He vented them, most narrow measure lent me;
> When the best hint was given him, he not took't,
> Or did it from his teeth. (III.iv.1–10)

He shows here that same jealous regard for his honor that lay behind his earlier temporizing with Octavius, and this might suggest that he is retreating into the old self-deception and paving the way for his long-intended return to Cleopatra. But this time he is not protesting too much, in view of his conduct since returning from Egypt. Shakespeare takes considerable pains to exclude the possibility that Antony is deceiving either himself or Octavia. In his familiar device of the "choric scene" (III.v), immediately following Antony's interview with Octavia, Shakespeare gives us Eros' independent, unprejudiced confirmation of Antony's case against Octavius. Instead of providing an ironic commentary on the pretentiousness or hypocrisy of the main characters, like the scene of Ventidius' victory in Parthia or the Fluellen episodes in *Henry V*, this choric scene provides information that amplifies and confirms Antony's argument. Eros reports that Caesar not only has made war on Pompey but has refused to share with Lepidus "the glory of the action"; that he has deposed Lepidus, and is about to have him executed. When Enobarbus asks him where Antony is at that moment, Eros replies:

> *Eros.* He's walking in the garden thus, and spurns
> The rush that lies before him; cries 'Fool Lepidus!'

And threats the throat of that his officer
That murd'red Pompey.

Eno.   Our great navy's rigg'd.

Eros.   For Italy and Caesar. (III.v.17–21)

Eros is reporting Antony's behavior *after* Octavia has left
to join her brother, when Antony is under no pressure to practice duplicity or self-deception. He reports Antony's shame at
his colleague's violation of their pact with Pompey, which had
been negotiated in the light of "strange courtesies and great"
that Pompey laid upon him. Eros is reporting as well Antony's
unaffected sorrow over the plight of Lepidus. In *Julius Caesar*
Antony called Lepidus "a slight unmeritable man,/ Meet to be
sent on errands"; and in this play he has made a laughing stock
of the drunken Lepidus at Pompey's banquet. But now in the
privacy of his garden, where he does not need to maintain
appearances, a transformed Antony laments and curses the fate
of Lepidus. Finally Eros gives us the crucial information that
even after Octavia's departure, Antony's navy is rigged "For
Italy and Caesar" and not for Egypt and Cleopatra. The sole
purpose of Eros' scene is to indicate that this time Antony's
scruples are genuine because earned.

An examination of Plutarch's version of this part of the
story suggests that Shakespeare intended that significance which
I have attributed to Eros' scene. In Plutarch's account, after
concluding the treaty with Pompey, Antony leaves his new wife
and launches the Parthian campaign. During that campaign
Cleopatra makes tempting gestures, and Antony responds with
what North calls his characteristic "effeminacy" by pursuing
Cleopatra. He is disloyal to Octavia almost from the moment
he marries her. Meanwhile Octavius tears up the treaty with
Pompey and sets out to recapture Sicily, with Antony's full
knowledge and even with the help of warships supplied by
Antony. Along the way Octavius deposes Lepidus. Antony goes
to Egypt, and from a throne mounted in the market place parcels
out the earth, the sun, and the moon among Cleopatra's children
and some minor potentates. For this Octavius denounces him

in Rome, and only in self-defense does Antony make charges against Octavius. Then he complains not that Octavius has broken faith in ruining Pompey and Lepidus but that he has refused to share with his accomplice Antony the spoils of victory.[2]

In transmuting just this much of Plutarch's narrative, Shakespeare improves Antony's moral position beyond recognition. He removes Antony from any contact with Cleopatra on the one hand and absolves him of any prior knowledge of Octavius' nefarious plans for Pompey and Lepidus on the other. He has Antony accuse Octavius first, in moral indignation rather than in self-defense: his charge is not that Octavius has denied him spoils but that Octavius has broken faith. And to forestall any suspicion that Antony is too prejudiced a spokesman in his own behalf, Shakespeare puts these accusations into the mouth of Eros. What Plutarch depicts as the sleazy conflict of two incompatibly rapacious appetites, in which "it was predestinated that the government of all the world should fall into Octavius Caesar's hands," Shakespeare purifies into a competition of honor won by Antony.

Shakespeare alters Plutarch even further, in order to cleanse Antony of shame in his relation with Octavia. In Plutarch's narrative Octavia mediates the differences that continually arise between Antony and Octavius, from the time of their renewed alliance against Pompey until the final outbreak of their civil war. She remains loyal to Antony despite his renewed liaison with Cleopatra and despite Octavius' ordering her to leave Antony's house. She exhibits the same solicitude for Fulvia's children as for her own, and she often intercedes with her brother on behalf of her husband. Her conduct is so impeccable that it does Antony unintended harm: "For her honest love and regard to her husband made every man hate him, when they saw he did so unkindly use so noble a lady." [3] Her loyalty is ended only when Antony himself sends word from Egypt that she is to leave his house.

In altering this part of Plutarch's account, Shakespeare has Antony conduct the Parthian campaign entirely through the agency of Ventidius, which leaves the impression that from the time of their marriage to the time of their parting at Athens, Antony and Octavia have never been separated. Despite Antony's earlier announcement that he made this marriage for his peace, the initiative and responsibility for their separation now fall upon Octavia, in typically ambiguous circumstances that nevertheless reflect no worse upon Antony than upon her. Informed of Antony's grievances against her brother, Octavia asks permission to go see Octavius and try to mend the quarrel. It is an admirable wish, but an untimely circumscription of her faith in Antony, since his grievances, if true, are not negotiable. At the time of their parting from Caesar, Antony had said of her,

> Her tongue will not obey her heart, nor can
> Her heart inform her tongue—the swan's down-feather
> That stands upon the swell at full of tide,
> And neither way inclines. (III.ii.47–50)

But now she inclines toward her brother willy-nilly, even if for an admirable purpose, out of the same statuesque hesitation between heart and tongue. Like Brutus' Portia, she exhibits a legalistic Roman impersonality just when it most behooves her as a wife to show a bit of Egyptian warmth. In effect if not in intention, she cannot credit Antony's grievances against Octavius until she can check up on them with Octavius himself; and it is not the least important function of Eros' choric scene to exhibit the shakiness of her position.

Antony's last words to Octavia, then, are those of a man who latterly has "kept his square" while everybody around him has been tracing hyperbolas:

> Gentle Octavia,
> Let your best love draw to that point which seeks
> Best to preserve it. If I lose mine honour,
> I lose myself. Better I were not yours
> Than yours so branchless. But, as you requested,
> Yourself shall go between 's. The mean time, lady,

> I'll raise the preparation of a war
> Shall stain your brother. Make your soonest haste;
> So your desires are yours. (III.iv.20–28)

And again:

> When it appears to you where this begins,
> Turn your displeasure that way, for our faults
> Can never be so equal that your love
> Can equally move with them. Provide your going;
> Choose your own company, and command what cost
> Your heart has mind to. (III.iv.33–38)

In the personal inflection of these lines there is nothing of the forced declamation that characterized Antony's earlier parting speech to Cleopatra or his reconciliation speech to Caesar. Here as in those earlier speeches, he is attending to his Roman honor. But this time his voice rings with conviction because this time his honor has been earned; and with the peerless tact, modesty, and confidence of a man who has had to undergo a reformation, who can no longer afford to be righteous unless he is right, he offers Octavia all possible help in making a journey that cannot help being an effrontery to him.

That effrontery, for all its noble motive, frees Antony for Egypt—not because it gives him a convenient excuse but because it measures his inner fulfilment of Roman honor against the external forms enacted by his wife and brother-in-law, and thus challenges him to make viable his Roman honor in an Egyptian life. Octavia here completes unwittingly what her brother began, the shrinking and localizing of those public values that Antony had come back to Rome in order to reconstruct and preserve. That her brother hardly expected in Antony a genuine renewal of honor is a less striking irony than that Octavia, the symbol of that renewal, should find herself unable to incline consistently toward Antony in his accomplishment. And the deepest irony is that only at the moment of her failure is Antony first able to voice the perception to which his conduct has led him, that it was only worth purging his Egyptian "effeminacy" in order to achieve the fullness of his Roman manhood:

> If I lose mine honour,
> I lose myself. Better I were not yours
> Than yours so branchless.

The "myself" to whom he refers is now the whole man acting out of conviction, not a self-deceived dotard rationalizing his honor. Antony's lines reflect his outgrowing of a world that thrives upon such shows; for his honesty and rectitude in the affairs of that world have given him a larger scope than either of its two chief inhabitants, his wife and brother-in-law. Their blindness to his honesty has left him to "stand up peerless" among the Romans, but it has absolved him of nothing. The play now frees him for Egypt, not to relapse into a familiar luxury, but to achieve on condition of his earned Roman honor that further ripeness which only the Nile generates. He is not left free to exchange one world for another; but by winning one world, he is enabled to reach for the other, to redeem each world through the other and make each one relevant to the other's glory.

III

Up through the end of Act III, scene v (Eros' choric scene), Shakespeare has located in Rome and its various adjuncts a total of eleven scenes comprising 863 lines, and in Egypt a total of six scenes comprising 606 lines. After Antony's departure from Egypt in I.iii, Shakespeare locates his remaining Egyptian scenes (I.v, II.vi, and III.iii) in places along the sequence that dramatize the contrast in tone, texture, and values between a Roman world whose ideal of rational, disinterested politics is uniquely capable of degenerating into the cynical bargaining of ward bosses, and an Egypt whose highest values of emotional fulfilment are equally capable of collapsing into mere willfulness and sybaritic vanity. This first half of the play, while presenting Antony's character and conflict, provides us also with a comparative anthropology of these two worlds, a running critique of the criteria of civilization as they are hammered out in the confrontation of the two cultures. Although this geographic polarization of values is rare in Shakespeare, there is nothing unfamiliar in the particular values represented by Rome and Egypt, nor in the fact of their opposition. They are, broadly speaking, the values of public and private life, of the state and the person, of honor and love; and the opposition of these values, along with the possibility of reconciling them, was one of Shakespeare's deepest concerns throughout his career, from the parallel battle scenes in *Henry VI* of a father killing his son and a son killing his father, to that moment in *The Tempest* when division is at last resolved and Gonzago announces that, despite all obstacles, Claribel has found a husband, Ferdinand a wife, Prospero a dukedom, ". . . and all of us ourselves/When no man was his own."

The public values of Rome arise from the same source as always in Shakespeare: the ideal of order, harmony, and mutuality in the state. At the beginning of the play Antony's lapsed honor is inseparable from the failure of the Roman peace, like two sides of a coin. To Antony's question on his return to Rome, "My being in Egypt,/Caesar, what was't to you?", in effect Caesar had already given an answer:

> If he fill'd
> His vacancy with his voluptuousness,
> Full surfeits and the dryness of his bones
> Call on him for't! But to confound such time
> That drums him from his sport and speaks as loud
> As his own state and ours—'tis to be chid
> As we rate boys who, being mature in knowledge,
> Pawn their experience to their present pleasure
> And so rebel to judgement. (I.iv.25–33)

These remarks could have been made about Richard II or about Prince Hal by his father. They remind us that this Roman tragedy, like *Julius Caesar* before it, is wrought from the same thematic materials as the cycle of chronicle plays from *Richard II* to *Henry V.* For they imply that same intimate connection between disorders of character and of the state, between personal honor and the public peace, that is the grand subject of the history plays.

But the public world of Rome and the values that serve it are placed in a different perspective from that of the history plays; and this difference is an important measure of Shakespeare's development during the period of his greatest works. I propose to examine that development in some detail, beginning with the history plays, in Chapters III and IV. It is enough to say here that England herself, the health and destiny of the nation, is the subject of those plays; and that the personalities and activities of individuals—Richard, Bolingbroke, Hotspur, and Prince Hal—are judged according to their actual or potential relation to the condition of England. The careers of men are conceived as subordinate to the general welfare. From the dying Gaunt's great paean to "This blessed land, this earth, this realm, this England," in *Richard II,* to King Henry V's battle cry before Harfleur, "God for Harry! England and St. George!", the integrity and glory of the nation is everywhere the criterion of individual conduct.

But Octavius in his speech doesn't mention Rome, doesn't refer even to a single community of which he and Antony both are members. The threat of Pompey is not, like that of Bolingbroke, Hotspur, and Macbeth, to an organic political society whose wholeness must be sustained by love, justice, and truth. It is a threat merely to "his own state and ours," to an accidental sum of wealth and power that has passed from the hands of Julius Caesar through those of his assassins, and now has accrued, "Like to a vagabond flag upon the stream," to the present triumvirs. In the design of the play the condition of Rome is subordinated to, and frequently obscured by, the interests and intrigues of persons. Before we pursue the sordid political implications of this fact, we must recognize also that in the design of the play Rome's security is guaranteed, regardless of the conduct and character of her citizens. In *Antony and Cleopatra* as in *Julius Caesar,* no matter how much our attention is focused abstractly upon politics, we are not permitted to fear concretely for the survival of the state. The urgencies we feel are on behalf of particular characters, irrespective of what happens to Rome. For Shakespeare and his audience the story of Rome was comfortably finished history, not a piece of uncertain ongoing business; and its symbolic meaning as history had already begun to reside in the stability of Roman political institutions.

In a variety of ways the two plays present Rome herself as the *donnée* rather than the protagonist of the drama—for example, the comic reassurance of Casca's jokes about Caesar refusing the crown three times in *Julius Caesar*, as contrasted with Owen Glendower's ostensibly comic but ominously unsettling insistence upon his astrological potency in *I Henry IV*. But the chief evidence of Rome's security is in the language itself: in *Julius Caesar* the name "Rome" becomes a personification, a term of familiar address woven into her citizens' discourse, so that we cannot imagine any limit to her life. Instead of asking God's blessing for Rome, these characters keep referring to Rome as a familiar household god:

Rome, thou has lost the breed of noble bloods! (I.ii.151)

What trash is Rome,
What rubbish and what offal, when it serves
For the base matter to illuminate
So vile a thing as Caesar! (I.ii.108–11)

By all the gods that Romans bow before,
I here discard my sickness! Soul of Rome!
Brave son, derived from honourable loins! (II.i.320–22)

Are yet two Romans living such as these?
The last of all the Romans, fare thee well!
It is impossible that ever Rome
Should breed thy fellow. (V.iii.98–101)

There is a certain easiness and relaxation of attitude toward a state that breeds and mourns, that alternately can be described as trash and given a soul. The multiplicity of forms and activities of which Rome is metaphorically capable makes it seem as continuous and indestructible as life itself. This personified conception of Rome is carried over into *Antony and Cleopatra*:

> He was dispos'd to mirth; but on the sudden
> A Roman thought hath struck him. (I.ii.86–87)

>   . . . with which I meant
> To scourge th' ingratitude that despiteful Rome
> Cast on my noble father. (II.vi.21–23)

> Contemning Rome, he has done all this and more
> In Alexandria. (III.vi.1–2)

>   Let Rome be thus
> Inform'd. (III.vi.19–20)

>   Sink Rome, and their tongues rot
> That speak against us! (III.vii.16–17)

> We'll bury him; and then, what's brave, what's noble,
> Let's do it after the high Roman fashion
> And make death proud to take us. (IV.xv.86–88)

In the verbal texture of these plays Rome is truly an Eternal City. Its internal divisions and civil wars themselves are evidence of its durability. They even swell its fortunes. Though Shakespeare did not write the two plays consecutively, there are many internal signs that he meant the political history of *Antony and Cleopatra* to pick up where *Julius Caesar* left off; and a striking fact about this continuity is that conspiracy and civil war seem not to have weakened the state but to have strengthened and enlarged it, until the triumvirs of Rome have become the triple pillars of the world.[4] The identification of Rome with the entire civilized world is pervasive in *Antony and Cleopatra*, and it frequently becomes explicit, as in Pompey's address to the triumvirs during the negotiations:

>   To you all three,
>   The senators alone of this great world,
>   Chief factors for the gods. . . (II.vi.8–10)

Rome has achieved a cosmic identity. Her political foundations have become so secure that her imagined destiny transcends the timeserving deeds of men. For Shakespeare's dramatic purpose Rome now becomes an idea, an abstract value with an almost allegorical significance. Having certified imaginatively the permanence of Rome as a political institution, Shakespeare is free to scrutinize the idea of Rome and to treat it as only one item in a pluralistic world of values.

Once he can do that, he attributes to Rome—pre-eminently in the person of Octavius Caesar—a political opportunism and a human mediocrity that amply confirm Cleopatra's final judgment, " 'Tis paltry to be Caesar." Octavius, a man essentially unmarked by malice or by love, is full of the cloistered virtue of the letter of the law. He is all but a cipher of the public world, a Roman Henry V, who, as the late Harold Goddard pointed out, is as quick to give up his sister for an empire as man ever was to give an empire for a whore.[5] He violates the pact with Pompey, deposes and executes Lepidus, and seeks every means to ruin Antony and insure Cleopatra's public humiliation. After rejecting Antony's challenge to personal combat and defeating him at Actium, he sends Thyreus to prey upon Cleopatra,

> From Antony win Cleopatra. Promise,
> And in our name, what she requires; add more,
> From thine invention, offers. Women are not
> In their best fortunes strong, but want will perjure
> The ne'er-touch'd Vestal. Try thy cunning, Thyreus.
> (III.xii.27–31)

and he repeatedly assures Cleopatra that he intends her no shame, only in order to preserve her from suicide so that he might lead her through Rome in triumph. " . . . feed, and sleep," he says to her at last, as if she were being fattened for lions. To be sure, Octavius is not so heartless as to remain untouched by the love and death of Antony and Cleopatra. When he hears of Antony's suicide, he says that "it is a tidings to wash the eyes of kings"; and when at last Cleopatra has frustrated

his designs by her suicide, nevertheless he orders her to be
buried with Antony in full solemnity. " . . . their story is/
No less in pity than his glory which/ Brought them to be
lamented," he says at the end. But these generous sentiments are
never permitted to qualify his political opportunism, as when,
his eyes freshly washed by the tidings of Antony's death, he
renews his effort to deceive Cleopatra so that she may be led
through Rome in triumph. He said of the dead Antony, "I must
perforce/ Have shown thee such a declining day,/ Or look on
thine," voicing a political theory that is conspicuous in Plutarch,
but which the play has shown is not in the least shared by
Antony.[6] The ideological rigidity of his commitment to this
theory is the principal source of Caesar's mischievous politics.

Octavius is only the play's most conspicuous example of
Roman opportunism and duplicity. In Menas, Pompey, and in
Antony himself, we have further evidence of degradation in
the political values of Rome. To Menas' grotesque plan for
cutting loose the ship on which the triumvirs are feasting and
then cutting their throats, Pompey makes a hypocritical reply
that is equally characteristic of Shakespeare's English and his
Roman plays:

> Ah, this thou shouldst have done,
> And not have spoken on't! In me 'tis villany;
> In thee 't had been good service. Thou must know,
> 'Tis not my profit that does lead mine honour;
> Mine honour, it. Repent that e'er thy tongue
> Hath so betray'd thine act. Being done unknown,
> I should have found if afterwards well done,
> But must condemn it now. Desist, and drink.
> (II.vii.79–86)

Antony's lieutenant Ventidius shows another facet of debased
Roman honor when, after his victory in Parthia, he explains
that although he can conquer still more territory for Antony,
Antony would become jealous if he did. He makes in advance
the necessary adjustment of Antony's profit to Antony's honor:
"Better to leave undone, than by our deed/ Acquire too high
a fame, when him we serve's away." (III.i.14–15)

This public world is naturally impatient of private feelings. Its calculating politics drain off the passions; and Octavius exemplifies its norm of temperament as well as its public practice. In his political efficiency he rejects everything personal, whether it is Antony's challenge to individual combat, or the reeling camaraderie of Pompey's banquet. Coupled with his devastating exposure of Roman pretensions in the banquet scene on Pompey's galley—both in the drunkenness of the celebrants and in Menas' plan for killing them—Shakespeare gives us a portrait of Octavius as nevertheless the most repellent Roman of them all. His superior restraint only enhances his unloveliness. This impersonality permeates his conduct throughout the play, from his reference to his sister as a "piece of virtue" that will "cement" him to Antony, to his desire to show his love for her publicly, "Which, left unknown,/ Is often left unlov'd," and finally to his effort to humiliate Cleopatra. Attempting to woo Cleopatra from Antony, Thyreus says of his master:

> But it would warm his spirits
> To hear from me you had left Antony
> And put yourself under his shrowd,
> The universal landlord. (III.xiii.69–72)

The juxtaposition of "warm . . . spirits," "shroud," and "universal landlord" implies a fundamental inhumanity that is Caesar's private counterpart to his political practice.

In this respect Octavia is unhappily her brother's sister. To all Romans but Enobarbus—to Octavius, Agrippa, Maecenas, Menas, and Antony himself—she is an ideal woman; and all share Maecenas' hope that her "beauty, wisdom, modesty, can settle/ The heart of Antony." We come to perceive and admire these virtues, and so does Antony. But they cannot settle his heart, because Octavia appeals only to that forensic fragment of himself that found its halting voice in the overblown rhetoric of his farewell to Cleopatra. Enobarbus explains with customary accuracy her incompatibility with Antony: "Octavia is of a holy, cold, and still conversation"; and her attempt to reconcile

Antony and Octavius, although it is nobly aimed at preserving peace in the family and the world, is inadequately grounded in loyalty to Antony and justifies the description.

Shakespeare's image of Rome, then, is variegated and complex, yet coherent. I have spoken of the degradation of Roman values; but behind that lies a high ideal of selfless devotion to the public good, a belief that honor, honesty, and order come before profit and pleasure, and that men must be loyal above all to those public duties that guarantee the human community. This ideal brings Antony back to Rome and prompts his marriage to Octavia. But behind the idealized public values is the suppression of private feeling and the cold impersonality of the political leader. This human inadequacy of the Roman ideal leaves Antony's marriage spiritually unconsummated and frees him for Egypt. At its worst the Roman ideal is perverted into Octavius' systematic spoliation of the world. At its best it produces the holy coldness of Octavia, in whom the breath of life has been diminished almost to nothing.

Cleopatra is set in deliberate contrast to Octavia, and Cleopatra is nothing less than Egypt and human feeling. She is all heat and motion and immoderate overflowing; she can barely be contained in loving, teasing, and then missing Antony, and is overwhelmed into a kind of madness by her jealousy of Octavia. She is truly the incarnation of private life, and she begins by regarding all public loyalties as forms of timeserving. She resists totally Antony's efforts to subject his personal life to public standards: she assumes that his Roman obligations are distracting and irrelevant to his life with her, and she is merely impatient to discover that "A Roman thought hath struck him." Later she will be schooled to the importance of public values, so that after Antony's death she chooses to kill herself "after the high Roman fashion." But at the beginning she balances Octavius and his sister by showing us both the perversion and the human inadequacy of merely private values.

In one sense Cleopatra is committed to the public world from the start, simply as Queen of the Nile. Like Richard II, Prince

Hal, and Julius Caesar, she is a public figure whether she likes it or not; and like them, she takes a histrionic satisfaction in her role. But she refuses to honor by word or deed the expectations of the public world. She uses her public status simply as an instrument of her pleasure and an extension of her privacy. She is selfish and spoiled, and she overcomes all obstacles to her desire simply by making the world her oyster. For one thing, she needs the world as a large enough stage to support her Alexandrian revels. Nothing less than the public eye can do justice to the scope and vitality of her private life, and all her pleasures (or almost all) are had in the open. In the play's first scene Antony proposes their evening's sport, not by inviting her to bed, but by reminding her of her wish to "wander through the streets and note/ The qualities of people." Later Enobarbus reports,

> I saw her once
> Hop forty paces through the public street;
> And having lost her breath, she spoke, and panted,
> That she did make defect perfection
> And, breathless, pow'r breathe forth. (II.ii.233 37)

and we never think to ask what was the occasion for this performance, for in Enobarbus' description the action justifies itself. Cleopatra and "the public street" are ornaments to each other, and they measure each other's value. In the same way the grandeur of her appearance at Cydnus, in Enobarbus' famous description, constitutes an autonomous value, since her perfumes and her fans and her mermaids command the homage of the city and of nature.

But however much Cleopatra lives her intimate life in the open air, private and public values do not meet and merge in her. Her beauty and passion vanquish all other considerations, and the public world exists simply to show her off. Cleopatra recognizes as a condition of her grandeur that she must outwit the world and bend it to her purpose. She devotes her intelligence and energy to cultivating those wily arts by which she can impose her interests upon the world and twist its great men around her fingers. The world must either be her plaything, as when she is ready to "unpeople" Egypt and fill the sea with messengers to express her passion for Antony, or it must be her enemy until it can be made her plaything.

From the beginning Egypt is her plaything, Rome her enemy. Whether the values of Rome are represented by Antony or Octavius, Enobarbus or Thyreus or Octavia, she deploys her cunning to subdue them to her will. When Antony has been struck by his "Roman thought" at the beginning of the play, she sets out to trick him in order to recapture his attention. At Actium she flees apparently out of fear; but her flight is also consistent with the strategy of beguilement by which she has ever tried to keep Antony from taking his honor too seriously. After the defeat at Actium she flirts with Thyreus, reminding him that she has had other lovers before Antony, and subtly implying that Caesar might be next. And she continues bargaining with Caesar, first through his underlings and then directly, even as she is tricking Antony into killing himself because of the false report of her death.

This wiliness of Cleopatra's is surely aimed at saving her own skin; but it has also a broader and more profound purpose. She is no less deceitful toward her lover than toward their common enemies, because she supposes that all public commitments, Antony's no less than Caesar's, threaten the integrity of her existence. She recognizes no distinction between the letter and the spirit of the Roman world, and until Antony's death she is blind to his growing difference from Octavius. At the beginning of the play she mocks Antony's Roman business, urging him to hear the messengers:

> Nay, hear them, Antony.
> Fulvia perchance is angry; or who knows
> If the scarce-bearded Caesar have not sent
> His pow'rful mandate to you: 'Do this, or this;
> Take in that kingdom, and enfranchise that.
> Perform't, or else we damn thee.' (I.i.19–24)

And near the end of the play, on the day of Antony's short-lived victory by land, she voices precisely the same attitude:

> Lord of lords!
> O infinite virtue, com'st thou smiling from
> The world's great snare uncaught? (IV.viii.16–18)

There is something oddly inappropriate in this response to Antony's victory. Almost all critics of the play, whatever their disagreements about other matters, regard the land battle as a moral triumph for Antony. Win or lose, do or die, Antony has momentarily overcome his weakness and stood up to the mark. But what we regard as a triumph Cleopatra considers a lucky escape; what we think is Antony's true and proper business she calls "the world's great snare." His "infinite virtue," for her, is something more than his having come off with his life: he has been "uncaught" spiritually as well as physically. He is smilingly aloof from his own victory.

There is evidence that Cleopatra has always expected Antony to take for granted her unremitting contempt for public values that threaten her comfort. She not only keeps betraying him but seems to assume that he should have expected her to do so, and not have taken offense. At Actium she insists upon participating in the battle, against the advice of Enobarbus and others, "as the president of my kingdom." But it is clear from everything we have learned about her, and from her conduct at Actium, that the entire function of the president of her kingdom is to become the object of universal gaze and wonder. Actium, like Cydnus, is for her a parade ground; and after the debacle she is surprised to discover that Antony supposed differently: "O my lord, my lord,/ Forgive my fearful sails! I little thought/ You would have followed." Her business at Actium was to cavort upon that stage where Antony made war. After the defeat she flirts with Thyreus not with the desire to betray Antony but only because she is Cleopatra; and again she is genuinely surprised that Antony should suspect her loyalty. To his charge that she has "mingled eyes" with Thyreus, she answers, "Not know me yet?"; and her magnificent speech that follows (III.xiii.158–67) indicates that this remark is in no way disingenuous.

Cleopatra dazzles us by her wild effort to personalize all of life and to vivify the world by her beauty and her passions. To our own time, which repeatedly compares itself regretfully to Rome, her celebration of the self, with all its recklessness, seems vastly preferable to all calculated claims to selfless public virtue. But her recklessness is finally self-destructive. It is not simply that in her antipathy to Rome she resorts to deceits and violence that subvert legitimate public values like honesty, loyalty, marriage, and public order, no less than Octavius ignores private values. Just as the ideal of Roman public life, carried far enough, becomes in Octavius the impersonal Machiavellian cynicism that is its opposite, so Cleopatra's persistence merely in private pleasure brings her to an inchoate restlessness where the self has no contour and therefore no substance. At the beginning of the play her quick shifts from mirth to sadness are designed to beguile only Antony. But in the three marvelous scenes where she is busy missing Antony, when she shifts from dreams of mandragora to dreams of former lovers, and from music to billiards to fishing, she is trying to beguile herself; and without the discipline of any commitment to those public values that have separated Antony from her, she is as unsuccessful with herself as she was with him. Her spirit can find no rest, and finally loses all coherence in venting itself upon the messenger who brings the news of Antony's marriage to Octavia. We find that outburst bewitching, perhaps, but only in the same uncomfortable way that we admire Octavius' sobriety at Pompey's banquet. For Cleopatra is doing violence not only to the messenger but to herself. In Cleopatra as in Octavius there is a surrender of human dignity, in him by an excessive self-control that stifles emotion, and in her by a failure of control that dissipates all emotion and causes Charmian to cry out, "Good madam, keep yourself within yourself,/ The man is innocent." Rome and Egypt truly require the discipline of each other. As I have suggested, that is the discipline Antony pursues; and later I will show how at the end of the play Cleopatra gleans it from him.

But now we must leave *Antony and Cleopatra* and explore the significant history of Shakespeare's long concern with the conflict of public and private values. In order to appreciate fully the significance of Shakespeare's resolution of the conflict in *Antony and Cleopatra*, ideally one should trace the development of the theme throughout his earlier plays. But the firm contours of that development are capable of being identified more briefly and selectively; and in this time-bound world I will confine myself to the cycle of history plays from *Richard II* to *Henry V*, to *Julius Caesar*, and to *Hamlet* and *King Lear*, a group of plays in which I believe Shakespeare enacted the larger part of his development.

CHAPTER THREE

THE EARLY HISTORY OF THE PUBLIC THEME:
THE IDEAL OF ORDER IN
THE HENRIAD AND *JULIUS CAESAR*

THE CONFLICT between public and private values is so conspicuous in *Antony and Cleopatra* that we might not be troubled by a statement that the play concerns the conflict. But we should balk at a similar statement about the history plays from *Richard II* to *Henry V*, for example, or about *Julius Caesar* or *Hamlet* or *King Lear*. In all these plays there is a division between public appearance and private reality; but that is only one among many aspects of each play, and in none is it the dominant aspect. The history plays and *Julius Caesar* are primarily concerned with the problem of order in society, with its ideal justification and its actual breakdown. In them the public-private discrepancy is adjunct to the main subject. *Hamlet* and *King Lear* are finally concerned with the nature of human identity and the structure of life itself. If they also deal with the relation between public and private values, that is because they are altogether comprehensive in scope.

Yet none of these plays is unique in its concerns, nor wholly alien to the others. In all of them various themes and motifs continuously overlap and feed into each other. To trace the background of *Antony and Cleopatra* in the earlier plays is to follow the shifting emphases and configurations among related ideas through a succession that we must not expect to culminate anywhere but at best to delimit and focus a major segment in Shakespeare's development.

The conflict between public and private values, which is to become an independent idea central to *Antony and Cleopatra*, first emerges in Shakespeare's history plays as a single aspect of the whole problem of order in society. We know that a belief in the correspondence of macrocosm and microcosm, the universe, the state, and the inner man, was pervasive in Elizabethan thought. This belief identifies personal disorder not simply with the existence of public disorder but also with the individual's particular failure to maintain public order, and his corresponding failure to integrate his public and private conduct. This integration becomes the ground of what we call "character." A man's inner differentiation is what gives him "character"; that differentiation takes its particular form in the way he relates his private to his public conduct, and his public conduct is measured by its capacity to defend the social order. In the world of correspondences, once the jarring of the social order calls public values into question, the whole relation of public to private values becomes immediately problematic, and with it the relation of man to himself—his character.

Antony and Cleopatra focuses upon the conflict within Antony between public and private claims at the microcosmic end of the scale, a conflict that reflects a macrocosmic disorder. But I have argued that for Antony there is no possibility of fusing the two claims, but only of finding a way to resolve their conflict by making them conditional to each other; and I have suggested that Shakespeare makes Rome symbolically superior to her momentary political fortunes, so that her destiny does not hang upon the thread of Antony's conduct. Now all of this implies that the play assumes a permanent discrepancy between the fate of the social order and that of the person. When Shakespeare makes Rome symbolically able to transcend her misfortunes and then consigns her fortunes to the paltry Caesar, he disconnects the problem of social order from Antony's personal conflict. This implies in turn the irrelevance of the doctrine of correspondences: from the point of view of that doctrine (though not of the play itself), Antony's problem of character is "beyond politics"; it must be faced independently of the fate of the social order, which is never truly at issue in the play. This implication, whose importance in understanding the play in its place in Shakespeare's development is enormous, will be elaborated in detail in later chapters. I touch on it here only to indicate the broad tendency of that development which we must now begin to trace in Shakespeare's history plays, where Shakespeare begins at the macrocosmic end of the scale with the dislocation of the social order, and where the doctrine of correspondences dominates his vision.

Shakespeare began his career, in the three parts of *Henry VI*, sharing the intense political concerns of his age, and eager to defend the official Tudor doctrine that political rebellion is never justified. The work of A. O. Lovejoy and E. M. W. Tillyard has familiarized us in detail with the ideology surrounding that doctrine.[1] Its principal tenets are (*a*) that the universe, the state, and the person are interdependently linked in one grand system of divinely sanctioned order; (*b*) that the internal structure and harmonious functioning of each single organism along this scale of being is parallel to, and contingent upon, the harmonious structure and function of all the others; (*c*) that this chain of being, with all its internal macrocosm-microcosm relationships, keeps the universe from relapsing into the chaos of Genesis 1:2; and hence (*d*) that man's mortal responsibility, as a unique creature capable of choice, is to sustain the whole creation, and at the same time to achieve his individuality within it, by keeping to his place and performing that particular function which constitutes his unique vocation. In performing his function, he cannot fear any restriction of his human possibility, because in the beautiful economy of the whole his human nature and his place in the system are perfectly integrated. What his place requires of him is precisely that he fulfil his own humanity. A king need not envy an angel because the pleasures of an angel are beyond his power to enjoy and because there are equivalent pleasures within his power. And so a cobbler need not envy a king, nor a skinned calf the cobbler.

But everybody's human possibility is threatened when anyone's place lapses, especially a keystone place like the king's.

Kings have a more comprehensive function than other men and are therefore more vulnerable. They can become weak or tyrannical, and in either case cut the cosmic chain and blight the human community. But attempts to restore health by overthrowing the king inevitably spread the disease and enlarge the range and duration of the cosmic malfunction. Two wrongs never make a right, disorder breeds disorder in geometrical rather than arithmetical progression, and therefore it is better to stand in one's place, to suffer what shocks our flesh is heir to, than to abandon one's identity by abdicating one's place and function. The misery people suffer from tyranny is always less than that which they suffer from rebellion and civil discord.

Shakespeare begins with the didactic promulgation of these doctrines. In the *Henry VI* trilogy he takes as his subject the recent history of political disorder well known to his audience, vivifies it with stage business, and moralizes it to fit the nervous political ideology of his time. Since his purpose is didactic and his adherence to the official ideology unqualified, the interest aroused by these plays is not fully dramatic but largely hortatory and polemical, like the interest produced by a dumb show. There is little room for the subtle, complex, and extensive delineation of character in relation to society that is to become one of the distinguishing marks of Shakespeare's greatness once he is willing to test dramatically the adequacy of the official ideology. Here the characters are treated simply as the atoms of cosmic friction, and Shakespeare feels no pressure to challenge, qualify, or elucidate the standard legends about their behavior or personalities. He is illustrating public doctrine, and it is sufficient for his purpose to present his characters only in their public aspect.

When he writes history plays again, in the *Henry IV* tetralogy, he moves backward in time for his subject and sharpens his focus upon the personal causes and results of political disorder. It is a striking fact that throughout his career Shakespeare keeps moving back (although somewhat irregularly) in his choice of historical subjects, not only within the framework of Tudor history, but from the matter of Tudor England to the matter of Rome, to an all but pre-national politics in *King Lear* and *Macbeth*, and finally to a symbolic equivalent for the beginning of human history in *The Tempest*. In thus moving backward, Shakespeare achieves both Olympian insight and detachment. He takes himself and his audience increasingly beyond the jurisdiction of local pride and prejudice, from the brittle affirmations of the patriotic pageant of *Henry VI* to a comprehensive exploration—through the resonant political thematics of his later tragedies and romances—of the possible relations of individual to society. He progressively simplifies his material as he discovers and generalizes what is typical in it, and thereby substitutes a concentrated analytical intensity, verging toward the complexity of symbolism, for a diffuse surface realism used to illustrate a simple ideological formula. The increasing range and depth of his art depend upon his ability to transcend, both in himself and his audience, the patriotic, cultish, and didactic sentiments inevitably aroused by the contemplation of what was for them recent English history, which had an unnerving capacity to repeat itself.

The first advantage of maturity that Shakespeare gains by moving backward into history is the ability to see the heroes of the past as persons rather than as the stock figures popularized by conventional ideology. The most striking innovation in the *Henry IV* cycle is Shakespeare's daring inquiry into the private life behind an accepted public legend; and this speculation takes its symptomatic form in the creation of Falstaff, a Lord of Misrule whose behavior endlessly affronts and parodies the standard ideal of order. Now Shakespeare takes for granted and leaves imbedded in his material the lesson he was so energetic to teach in his earliest plays: the idea that kingship is a vocation of love that unites mankind, but that political rebellion can only deepen the failure of that vocation, is amply illustrated by the events leading from the rebellion against Richard II to the restoration of political order by Henry V. That idea, with the events that embody it, now becomes a means and not an end, the *donnée* of the drama, a pattern so familiar that without being slighted it may be left in the background.

The foreground is devoted to Shakespeare's dramatic rendering of the private counterpart of public action, the motives and anxieties, the hopes aroused, and the denials required by man's effort to fulfil his appointed place in the order of the world.

In this surgical uncovering of the personal history behind the public history, Shakespeare first achieves the psychological and ethical insight for which we celebrate him. The *Henry IV* tetralogy begins that great venture in the psychological drama that will produce his most beautifully wrought plays and his profoundest moral vision. Behind that venture is the catalytic perception, in the materials of the chronicle play, of a discrepancy between public and private life, and behind that perception is a willingness to question for the first time the human adequacy of the traditional ideology. Shakespeare frees himself from the didacticism of the tradition because now he needs to dramatize the conflict between public and private behavior as a central aspect of the problematic character of the accepted doctrine of order.

A frequently discussed passage from T. S. Eliot is especially useful in explaining this development. Speaking of the motives for Othello's final speech, Mr. Eliot says:

> What Othello seems to me to be doing in making this speech is cheering himself up. He is endeavouring to escape reality, he has ceased to think about Desdemona, and is thinking about himself. Humility is the most difficult of all virtues to achieve; nothing dies harder than the desire to think well of oneself. Othello succeeds in turning himself into a pathetic figure, by adopting an *aesthetic* rather than a moral attitude, dramatizing himself against his environment. He takes in the spectator, but the human motive is primarily to take in himself. I do not believe that any writer has ever exposed this *bovarysme,* the human will to see things as they are not, more clearly than Shakespeare.[2]

Reality, Mr. Eliot implies, demands a moral rather than an aesthetic attitude, public rather than private; but if Othello were to adopt the moral attitude required, he could no longer think well of himself. Hence he abandons reality in order to appease his vanity.

I think Mr. Eliot is wrong about Othello but right about Shakespeare: the psychic process he describes is familiar even to readers of the plays who are not steeped in Freud. What needs to be emphasized is that in Mr. Eliot's formulation, the new "self-consciousness and self-dramatization of the Shakespearean hero," which reflects "not a very agreeable" stage of human history, is governed by a recognizable external reality; and this reality, because it demands moral attitudes, is the source and standard of moral judgment. "Reality," in this context, is a difficult word to understand. It must comprise at the very least a coherent set of ethical values by which to measure particular instances of departure or escape. In actual life this criterion is provided by the historical spirit of the age and the custom of the country; but in a play, where "reality" must be given a more vivid shape, it is most readily compressed into the created image of a public world peculiar to the play.

The public world of Shakespeare's history plays incorporates in its "reality" the traditional doctrines of order by which Richard II and Prince Hal are to be judged. Their self-deceptions, then, are not random expressions of temperament but specific responses to particular conflicts with the reality of the social order represented in the plays. In *Richard II* Shakespeare shows a character temperamentally unable to meet the demands of his society, who nevertheless imagines himself to have accomplished already what in fact he is unable to begin, the proper ordering and defense of his kingdom. Richard, who seems to interest Shakespeare just in so far as he is temperamentally unfit to discharge his royal vocation, thinks himself the very model of a king, with angels in his service. In *Henry IV* the demands of society deny basic human needs, which then must be supplied by self-dramatization. Prince Hal is asked to be a king and no king, to behave as a proper prince but to remain in his father's shadow. When he prefers instead to "make offence a skill" and stake out his own claim by acting like a naughty boy, we cannot easily blame him for wanting more human space than the narrow "reality" of his world allows. And in *Julius Caesar* the character finds his society unable to live up to his hopes for it, and yet manages to persuade himself that he is satisfied. Betrayed by Cassius into betraying his own "best lover," and then again by the Antony whose life he had saved, Brutus says at Philippi: "Countrymen,/ My heart doth joy that yet in all my life/ I found no man but he was true to me."

From *Richard II* to *Antony and Cleopatra* Shakespeare's analysis of human character, with its conspicuous element of self-dramatization, is inseparable from his exploration of the conflict between public and private values. In *Antony and Cleopatra* that conflict is oriented geographically between Rome and Egypt as well as psychologically within the hero's character. In the earlier plays it is almost entirely an internal conflict. And in his portrayals of Richard, Hal, Brutus, Hamlet, Othello, Lear, Macbeth, and Antony, we witness a progressive diminution in the self-deception with which Shakespeare invests his characters, and with it his growing perception that the authoritarian public philosophy with which he began cannot remain the whole foundation of human existence. By tracing in the earlier plays Shakespeare's manner of relating self-dramatization to the conflict of public and private values, we may follow the process by which he outgrows the public philosophy and works himself through the intellectual history of *Antony and Cleopatra*.

II

Clearly, Richard II has a histrionic flair, which might have begun as a mere temperamental eccentricity: in the lists at Coventry, having taken his central part in the gorgeous ceremony of announcing the contestants, he calls off the duel just as the spotlight is ready to shift from himself to them. But in the play his theatricality is continually related to the pressures of the public world. When Richard fails to persuade Mowbray and Bolingbroke to obey him and make peace, then proudly announces "We were not born to sue, but to command," and then commands them to do just what he does not want them to do, his self-dramatization enables him to overlook his inability to discharge his office truly. As his political fortunes deteriorate, he needs all the more to hide from himself both his past mistakes and his continuing indecisiveness; and in a familiar series of speeches after Bolingbroke's return from exile, Richard evokes an image of himself that performs this function. He creates by his rhetoric those pathetic circumstances that arouse our sympathy even while they distract us, as they do him, from besetting political perils that are impervious to rhetoric.

Richard's irresponsibility has made him vulnerable to Bolingbroke and his supporters; and Bolingbroke's return forces Richard to face up to his vocation for the first time. But he seeks neither to defend his mistakes, to undo them, nor to ignore them and negotiate freshly with Bolingbroke. He is so blinded by his image of himself that he is aware neither of having erred in the past nor of having to take swift action now:

> Not all the water in the rough rude sea
> Can wash the balm off from an anointed king.
> The breath of worldly men cannot depose
> The deputy elected by the Lord.
> For every man that Bolingbroke hath press'd
> To lift shrewd steel against our golden crown,
> God for his Richard hath in heavenly pay
> A glorious angel. Then, if angels fight,
> Weak men must fall; for heaven still guards the right.
> (*Richard II*, III.ii.54–62)

Here Shakespeare begins his radical scrutiny of the conventional doctrine by putting it into the mouth of just that man who has failed to validate the doctrine by his deeds. Richard dramatizes himself as one whose status cannot be affected by his conduct, as the formal proprietor rather than the active defender of that glorious England which has been the subject of Gaunt's dying speech. Angels will defend him, not he them, simply because his place in the world is inviolable.

Later, when the initiative and advantage have passed unmistakably to Bolingbroke, Richard merely exchanges his delusion of divine power for one of hapless impotence. In the scene at Flint Castle where Bolingbroke stands in the "base court" while Richard emerges on the walls above, Bolingbroke begins humbly enough, acknowledging Richard as God's anointed:

> See, see, King Richard doth himself appear,
> As doth the blushing discontented sun
> From out the fiery portal of the East
> When he perceives the envious clouds are bent
> To dim his glory and to stain the track
> Of his bright passage to the Occident.
> *(Richard II,* III.iii.62–67)

In his comparison of Richard to the sun and of himself to an "envious cloud" (which anticipates exactly the language of Prince Hal's soliloquy), Bolingbroke employs a conventional analogy to show his acquiescence in Richard's divine claims for himself. Bolingbroke then bends his knee in obeisance, and through Northumberland demands only the restitution of the Lancastrian estates. Richard begins the negotiation promisingly, affirming that he is God's steward on earth, prophesying death and destruction if arms are lifted against him, and offering to satisfy Bolingbroke's legitimate demands. But Richard cannot maintain his royal poise even long enough for Northumberland to return with Bolingbroke's reply. Without waiting for an answer, the man who has just insisted upon his heavenly stewardship says:

> What must the King do now? Must he submit?
> The King shall do it. Must he be depos'd?
> The King shall be contented. Must he lose
> The name of king? A God's name, let it go!
> I'll give my jewels for a set of beads,
> My gorgeous palace for a hermitage,
>
> .   .   .   .
>
> Most mighty prince, my Lord Northumberland,
> What says King Bolingbroke? Will his Majesty
> Give Richard leave to live till Richard die?
> You make a leg, and Bolingbroke says ay.
> *(Richard II,* III.iii.143–75)

The very act of negotiating is fatal to his sense of divinity, and his image of himself is finally dearer to him than his divine office. For the man who addressed England as "my earth" to bargain with an illegally returned exile would destroy his delusion of grandeur, even if the bargain completed would enable him to call the earth his. Richard prefers to exchange his delusion, yet intact, for another while there is still time. In a breath hardly longer than that which took four years off Bolingbroke's banishment, he transforms himself from the proprietor of "my earth" to the despised and rejected inhabitant of a six-foot plot.

Richard continues with a series of speeches that elaborate this pathetic image, as when he compares himself to Christ betrayed by Judas and sent by Pilate to his "sour cross." Richard is surely a precursor of Hamlet in his habit of generalizing from his situation to the condition of man. But there is a striking difference between them. Hamlet, however widely his mind ranges in searching out the sources and analogues of his situation, never forgets for long the task and its dangers that have been laid upon him. His doubt and delay are necessary to find a coherent plan of legitimate action. But he knows he cannot wait indefinitely for such a plan, and meanwhile he makes a number of oblique and abortive thrusts at his adversary. Even as he waits and generalizes, he is continuously improvising action. Hamlet is after all one of Shakespeare's busiest characters.

But Richard is idle; he generalizes his situation in order to get his mind off it and avoid all action. He does not shrink from a particular unexpected task but from that continuing labor which his royal being requires of him, the defense of his kingdom. Wholly unlike Hamlet, he shrinks from the very idea of action. From the moment of his return from Ireland he does nothing but speak, and from moment to moment he speaks whatever part is most flattering to him, whether or not the part he speaks will save himself or his kingdom. The Duke of York characterizes accurately, if unwittingly, this histrionic tendency in his description of Richard's final humiliation in Bolingbroke's coronation procession:

As in a theater the eyes of men,
After a well-grac'd actor leaves the stage,
Are idly bent on him that enters next,
Thinking his prattle to be tedious,
Even so, or with much more contempt, men's eyes
Did scowl on gentle Richard. . . .
(*Richard II*, V.ii.23–28)

The last and most painful irony in Richard's downfall is that even in the pageantry of kingship that he loves best of all, the actor must yield to the man of action. Richard gets contempt instead of applause while Bolingbroke, who is indifferent to the pageantry so long as he has the power, steals the show as well as the scepter.

Shakespeare never again creates a character whose self-dramatization is so elaborate and unqualified as Richard's. But Prince Hal, to the success of whose career Shakespeare is committed by his sources and by the irresistible expectations of his audience, still is invested with a self-dramatization peculiarly defined by his delicate public status in the two parts of *Henry IV*. Hal's legendary waywardness, represented in the play by his tavern life, is directed by Shakespeare to a crucial dramatic purpose. To be sure, the distance from the Boar's Head Tavern to the court indicates the momentary difference between Hal's dissoluteness and his brother Lancaster's precocious involvement in public affairs; but it also measures the difference between Hal's political innocence and the taint of his father's guilt in acquiring the throne. The Boar's Head Tavern lies conveniently outside the perimeter of guilt that encompasses both the king and the Percies; and Shakespeare's portrayal of Hal's waywardness is a way of keeping him politically unsoiled.

The tavern is nevertheless a low hangout for a prince; if it protects Hal from his father's guilt, it also threatens him from another direction. Hal is aware of this danger, and attempts to cope with it in his soliloquy at the end of I.ii:

I know you all, and will awhile uphold
The unyok'd humour of your idleness.
Yet herein will I imitate the sun,

Who doth permit the base contagious clouds
To smother up his beauty from the world,
That, when he please again to be himself,
Being wanted, he may be more wond'red at
By breaking through the foul and ugly mists
Of vapours that did seem to strangle him.
If all the year were playing holidays,
To sport would be as tedious as to work;
But when they seldom come, they wish'd-for come,
And nothing pleaseth but rare accidents.
So, when this loose behaviour I throw off
And pay the debt I never promised,
By how much better than my word I am,
By so much shall I falsify men's hopes;
And, like bright metal on a sullen ground,
My reformation, glitt'ring o'er my fault,
Shall show more goodly and attract more eyes
Than that which hath no foil to set it off.
I'll so offend to make offence a skill,
Redeeming time when men think least I will.
                    (*Part I*, I.ii.219–241)

The soliloquy follows immediately Hal's opening scene with Falstaff and his decision to join in the Gadshill robbery, and it is clearly intended to assuage our anxiety about Hal's moral status. It relaxes us so that we may surrender ourselves to the comedy of the robbery and its aftermath, secure in the expectation that Hal will emerge from his adventure a still uncompromised candidate for the throne. Beyond this, however, the dramatic significance of the soliloquy has been much debated; and here I stand with those who argue that Hal is cheering up not only the audience but himself as well. The soliloquy, says Dr. Johnson, in words that anticipate Mr. Eliot's stricture on Othello, "exhibits a natural picture of a great mind offering excuses to itself, and palliating those follies which it can neither justify nor forsake." [3] It exhibits the same histrionic self-consciousness, the impulse to peep at oneself over one's shoulder, that is conspicuous in Richard. By making offense a skill, Hal can keep always in the spotlight. He can achieve a unique personal notoriety, in the court by what is considered his dissoluteness, then in the tavern by a condescension that the commoners (except Falstaff, who understands better than Hal its complex motive) praise as princely, and then again in the court by a miraculous and perfectly timed reformation. Meanwhile he can indulge his appetite for repartee with Falstaff, and he can participate with the fat knight in a biting exposure of the hypocritical pretensions of the noble characters who, unlike himself, have King Richard on their consciences. Like Richard, although for different reasons, Hal is out of touch with his public function. Unlike Richard, he will perform that function eagerly and well once his time comes. But he is unavoidably separated from it now, and like Richard, he elaborates an image of himself whose purpose is to bridge the gap between his exalted function and his present remoteness from it.

Hal's image of himself is more calculated than Richard's, and it is to be infinitely more successful in serving his ends. But his ends are no less vain in their way than Richard's; and much of Hal's conduct in both parts of *Henry IV* confirms the histrionic impression created by his opening soliloquy. He keeps policing his image of himself, with his eyes on us as we watch him. Several times in the tavern he obliquely proposes the justification for his conduct that it is necessary to the proper education of an enlightened prince, teaching him the democratic capacity to "drink with any tinker in his own language during my life," and at the same time winning his future subjects' loyalty by his genial appearance among them. But the meaning of his descent into the wine cellar of the tavern, where he sounds "the very bass-string of humility" with the drawers Tom, Dick, and Francis, is strongly qualified in *Part II* by his revealing "small beer" scene (II.ii) with Poins. Since this scene marks Hal's first appearance in *Part II*, it is striking that immediately he announces himself "exceeding weary." When Poins is surprised that weariness should descend upon one of royal blood, Hal replies:

> *Prince.* Faith, it does me, though it discolours the complexion of my greatness to acknowledge it. Doth it now show vilely in me to desire small beer?

Poins. Why, a prince should not be so loosely studied as to remember so weak a composition.

Prince. Belike then my appetite was not princely got; for, by my troth, I do now remember the poor creature, small beer. But indeed these humble considerations make me out of love with my greatness. What a disgrace is it to me to remember thy name! or to know thy face to-morrow! or . . .

(*Part II*, II.ii.5-16)

There is something warm, intimate, and touching about Hal at such a rare moment. He steps ever so slightly out of the formulated role in which he has cast himself, to express with some candor those feelings that have had no room to show in the image of one who makes offense a skill. In conceiving his greatness as a palpable end in itself, with its own complexion to be fallen in and out of love with, Hal exhibits again that pervasive self-consciousness that puts life at one remove and makes it ancillary to his image of himself. But his opening expression of weariness, followed so quickly by the dialogue quoted, is surely a confession of the expense of spirit it has cost him to contain himself within that image and to keep life in abeyance. Moreover, he now worries that the tavern conduct that he previously claimed was admirable in its democratic humility has in fact revealed him as indifferent to his responsibilities; and this implies a profound doubt that his original strategy has been successful. In effect, Hal is saying that he has exhausted himself playing the role announced in his soliloquy, and even so that his energy perhaps has been wasted: he still *shows* vilely, so that the audience he has addressed might think his prattle to be tedious after all. But he does not stop even here. He wonders also whether "my appetite was not princely got," and thereby reveals for a moment the possibility that his elaborate strategy has enabled him so far to evade. Perhaps, he admits, the desire for small beer has been all along not a piece of strategy but a proof of character! Perhaps, indeed, his rhetoric has taken in himself as well as his intended audience.

Hal proceeds to a punning speech on Poins's linen that exhibits again his Falstaffian appetite for banter, and leads Poins to chide him for idle chatter while his father is sick. Under this renewed pressure Hal retreats immediately into his customary attitude and explains that he is privately full of grief over his father's illness, but that he would be thought a hypocrite to show that grief publicly. As Leonard Unger has shown, in an essay to which my analysis of these plays is everywhere indebted,

> His [Hal's] sentiments here are convincing, but not his logic. He would rather be thought a waster and a heartless son than a hypocrite. He is more concerned with what men like Poins think than with what his father thinks. It would be out of character. He will weep when he is ready to step out of that character into another, when he performs the somersault of reformation, when he and the time are ready for him to put his heart into the act and the crown on his head. Then *he* will not think himself a hypocrite, and that is what matters.[4]

In the "small beer" scene as in his opening soliloquy, Hal is playing to himself as well as to us; he is shaping an image of himself that will accommodate his private appetite for Falstaffian potluck and still leave open a princely path to public power; and inevitably he deceives himself amidst his efforts to deceive others.

Hal exhibits his characteristic self-consciousness once more conspicuously, in the scene (*Part II,* IV.v.) where he mistakes his father's sleep for death and tries on the crown for size, gets caught red-handed when his father wakes up unexpectedly, and is so eloquent in explaining that he has only been coming to terms with the crown "as with an enemy" that his father decides on his deathbed that Hal has made offense a skill in order to make reform a greater skill. Once his father is dead and Hal emerges at last from his parasitical status in his world, he is no longer under the pressure toward self-deception. He is ready to enter upon his life at last, and to abandon his now outworn image of himself by disowning Falstaff:

> I know thee not, old man. Fall to thy prayers.
> How ill white hairs become a fool and jester!

> I have long dreamt of such a kind of man,
> So surfeit-swell'd, so old, and so profane;
> But being awak'd, I do despise my dream.
>
> . . . .
>
> When thou dost hear I am as I have been,
> Approach me, and thou shalt be as thou wast,
> The tutor and the feeder of my riots.
> Till then I banish thee, on pain of death,
> As I have done the rest of my misleaders,
> Not to come near our person by ten mile.
>
> *(Part II,* V.v.51–69)

The tavern life, which he once claimed was part of his democratic education, he now blames on his misleaders; and that
offense which he cultivated as a skill, now he disowns as
a dream. Both Plato and Freud agree that in dreams begin
*ir*responsibilities: when Hal newly crowned no longer needs a
substitute notoriety, he quickly dissociates himself from the
play-within-a-play initiated by his opening soliloquy.

The self-dramatization of Richard and Hal is coextensive
with their failure to perform the public office that is their vocation, Richard through ineptness, Hal through strategic choice.
Richard's self-dramatization is immediately self-destructive; and
the destruction does not spare those regally poetic elements in
his temperament that, despite his self-deception, continue to
compel our admiration. Hal's self-dramatization is fruitlessly
circular for himself, as indicated by his confession in the "small
beer" scene, and destructive to others: having played the politics
of the tavern rather than the court, he has kept Richard off his
conscience only to put Falstaff on it. And there is also a self-
destructive element in the rejection of Falstaff. "Banish plump
Jack, and banish all the world," the fat knight had told him;
in the end we see Hal banish in himself that Falstaffian appetite
for the world which, though it "was not princely got," constantly surprised and delightfully reassured us by its shared
and supple humanity. In those last unsettling lines, "I banish
thee . . . / Not to come near our person by ten mile," the
shift from the open language of "I" and "thee" to the cold
formality of the royal "we" reminds us that Hal must pay a

high price for his success, perhaps as high as Richard paid in failure. We must recognize in any case that both in Richard's failure and Hal's success some important human potentialities have failed of actualization; and hence that the world Shakespeare has put them in, the public world of the traditional ideology of order, in some measure damns its heroes as well as its failures. The impotent circularity of self-dramatization in Richard and Hal measures the inadequacy of their world to accommodate private values. At a very deep level of his imagination, Shakespeare challenges here the doctrine that had contented him before; and to trace his growing doubt, we must turn now from the characters to their ethical environment, that "reality" in the face of which they are compelled to dramatize themselves in fragmented images that stifle essential facets of their humanity.

III

There is ample reason to regard the four plays from *Richard II* to *Henry V* as a single work of the imagination, above all in their rendition of a complete political cycle from order through disorder to reunification under an ideal king.[5] That cycle illustrates the traditional doctrine: the deposition of Richard leads to greater violence and discord than England had to suffer under the tyranny of Richard's weakness; and political harmony is restored only by one who is free both of Richard's weakness and of any taint of guilt for Richard's deposition.

England herself is the heroine of the action, and she is described magnificently by one who loves her in Gaunt's speech at the beginning of the cycle:

> This royal throne of kings, this scept'red isle,
> This earth of majesty, this seat of Mars,
> This other Eden, demi-paradise,
> This fortress built by Nature for herself
> Against infection and the hand of war,

> This happy breed of men, this little world,
> This precious stone set in the silver sea,
> Which serves it in the office of a wall,
> Or as a moat defensive to a house,
> Against the envy of less happier lands;
> This blessed plot, this earth, this realm, this England,
> This nurse, this teeming womb of royal kings,
> Fear'd by their breed and famous by their birth,
> Renowned for their deeds as far from home,
> For Christian service and true chivalry,
> As is the sepulchre in stubborn Jewry
> Of the world's ransom, blessed Mary's son;
> This land of such dear souls, this dear dear land,
> Dear for her reputation through the world,
> Is now leas'd out (I die pronouncing it)
> Like to a tenement or pelting farm.
>   (*Richard II,* II.i.40–60)

That is as passionately moving in tone as patriotic utterance can be; and we do not hear this tone again until the end of the cycle, when England's restorer and champion, King Henry V, rouses his armies to battle in France:

> This day is call'd the Feast of Crispian.
> He that outlives this day, and comes safe home,
> Will stand a-tiptoe when this day is nam'd
> And rouse him at the name of Crispian.
> He that shall live this day, and see old age,
> Will yearly on the vigil feast his neighbors
> And say 'To-morrow is Saint Crispian.'
> Then will he strip his sleeve and show his scars,
> And say 'These wounds I had on Crispin's day.'
> Old men forget; yet all shall be forgot,
> But he'll remember, with advantages,
> What feats he did that day. . . . (*Henry V,* IV.iii.40–51)

The tiptoe country of neighborly feasting is neither leased out nor torn by dissension within. There King Henry's "happy few" may grow old quietly among his grandfather's "happy breed." His grandson sets right the broken political harmony that Gaunt died to witness, and earns in action the lovingly tuned rhetoric that echoes England's glory. The traditional ideology of order is justified not as an empty form but as the guarantor of peace and yearly feasting in a dear land.

The patriotic devotion expressed in these plays is surely not false or cynical. Shakespeare celebrates with profound conviction the glory of England and of the ideal king who restores her. But he begins to doubt by implication that the doctrine of order embraces an inclusive and ultimate human value. He begins to see its incapacity to fulfil the promise that every man may have his full human scope within the limits of place and vocation assigned him by the cosmic system, and hence the insufficiency of the doctrine, given man's restless powers of creation and destruction, to guarantee the undisturbed continuity of human society. The fruitless self-dramatizations of Richard and Prince Hal are symptoms of this failure; in *Henry V,* the play that celebrates the ideal king in his vocation, Shakespeare gives us the direct evidence. We must put alongside King Henry's gorgeous utterances at Harfleur and Agincourt his equally familiar speech on Ceremony, in which he expresses a weariness with his vocation comparable to Prince Hal's in the "small beer" scene:

> Upon the king! Let us our lives, our souls,
> Our debts, our careful wives,
> Our children, and our sins, lay on the King!
> We must bear all. O hard condition,
> Twin-born with greatness, subject to the breath
> Of every fool, whose sense no more can feel
> But his own wringing! What infinite heart's-ease
> Must kings neglect that private men enjoy!
> And what have kings that privates have not too,
> Save ceremony, save general ceremony?
> And what art thou, thou idol Ceremony?
> What kind of god art thou, that suffer'st more
> Of mortal griefs than do thy worshippers?
> What are thy rents? What are thy comings-in?
> O Ceremony, show me but thy worth!
> What is thy soul of adoration?
> Art thou aught else but place, degree, and forms,
> Creating awe and fear in other men?
>
> (*Henry V,* IV.i.247–64)

This long speech on Ceremony, of which I have quoted only the opening lines, comes at the end of a scene in which King Henry has gone disguised among the common soldiers on the eve of Agincourt, and found them lacking in enthusiasm for his cause. We are reminded that in the opening scenes of the play Shakespeare took pains to present that cause ambiguously: the churchmen who vindicated Henry's French claims might be accused of thereby diverting him from a threatened confiscation of church property, just as his father had wished to undertake foreign wars to divert attention from the domestic broils that brought him questionably to the throne. In giving this credence to the common soldiers' doubts, Shakespeare has come a long way from the Jack Cade scenes of *Henry VI*. He has made clear, moreover, King Henry's failure to achieve that command of all the lads in Eastcheap which had been the professed aim of Prince Hal's tavern education in *Henry IV*. That King Henry in this play is a different sort of person from Prince Hal is no accident. His purpose in going among the common soldiers, to be sure, is like Prince Hal's in the tavern: again he wishes to engage "with any tinker in his own language." But now that he is reformed, neither his language nor his cause is so hospitably human as before; and on the subject of the king's war, he finds little common ground with his soldiers. His adventure ends with a different sort of engagement than he anticipated: an exchange of gauntlets with the soldier Williams.

The speech on Ceremony, then, is no set piece of bravura dropped into the play at an odd moment but the logical and probable outcome of the king's encounter with the common soldiers. It proclaims a gulf between public and private life that can no longer be bridged by any sort of role-playing and reduces the sacramental structure of "place, degree, and form" to the mere façade of Ceremony. England herself may inspire love; but the king who champions her, despite his efforts to cement by that love the organic interdependence of her people, concludes on good evidence that he must sacrifice his own heart's ease in order to hold them in place, and then only by fear. Public and private purposes are not only severed from each other but each is left unconsummated on its own terms.

The speech on Ceremony is followed shortly by the Battle of Agincourt, where Shakespeare yet takes pains to keep reminding us of the "mortal griefs" connected with the ceremonies of the public world. After it is clear that the battle will go to the English, King Henry is told of the deaths of York and Suffolk, and then hears an alarum sounded by the French. He says:

> But hark! what new alarum is this same?
> The French have reinforc'd their scatter'd men.
> Then every soldier kill his prisoners!
> Give the word through. (*Henry V*, IV.vi.35–38)

The king's apparent rationale, that the English may properly kill their prisoners simply because the French have regrouped their forces, in fact does not do justice to his actual provocation. Fluellen will tell us in the next scene that the French violated the law of war by raiding the English supply tents behind the lines and killing the servant boys left there, and that the king's order to kill the French prisoners, here as in Holinshed, is a retaliation for that wanton cruelty.[6] But we cannot help remembering an earlier and, so to speak, happier war, which was indeed precipitated by Hotspur's insistence upon withholding his prisoners, but which was consummated by Prince Hal's magnanimity in freeing his prisoner. That magnanimity, the gay aplomb by which Prince Hal could let Falstaff claim credit for killing Hotspur even while he himself set Douglas free, and thereby garner his glory in every quarter at once, has no place in this new world. And as if to underscore the contrast between Prince Hal and King Henry, Shakespeare follows the king's order to kill the French prisoners with a heavily ironic scene between Fluellen and Gower. Having bemoaned the murder of the English boys and praised the king for his order to kill the French prisoners, Fluellen, full of Welsh pride over the king's birth at Monmouth, launches into a panegyric comparing King Henry to Alexander the Great. Fluellen reaches his climax just fifty lines after the king's order to kill the prisoners:

Fluellen. . . . As Alexander kill'd his friend Cleitus, being in his ales and his cups, so also Harry Monmouth, being in his right wits and his good judgements, turned away the fat knight with the great-belly doublet. He was full of jests, and gipes, and knaveries, and mocks. I have forgot his name.

Gower. Sir John Falstaff.

Fluellen. That is he. I'll tell you there is good men porn at Monmouth.

Gower. Here comes his majesty.

(*Henry V*, IV.vii.44–56)

And the king comes onstage repeating his order. Not the least element in the multiple irony here is that Alexander was drunk when he killed his friend, whereas Henry "in his right wits and good judgements" turned away Falstaff. Fluellen, for all his charm, is used throughout the play to provide ironic commentary upon the king's conduct. His function is like that of Falstaff and Prince Hal in *Henry IV;* and Shakespeare is almost too mechanical in making him remind us sympathetically of Falstaff just at that moment when the king must deliver himself over to the anger and cruelty sometimes required by the vocation from which Falstaff threatened to mislead him. With the rejection of Falstaff and the slaughter of French prisoners deliberately juxtaposed in our minds, we cannot help questioning the public values that require these expenditures of life, and hence the whole ideology ostensibly being vindicated by the play.

But I think there is both a subtler and a more profound way in which Shakespeare now suggests the human limitations of that ideology. It is easy enough at any time to be ironic about war; and in this respect Fluellen's function is a good deal more perfunctory, say, than Falstaff's when the fat knight delivers his catechism on honor. Shakespeare now goes on to exhibit the same reduction of the king's range in wooing as in war. The scene of King Henry's courting Katherine of France provides the play's great occasion for him to encompass the highest private value of married love in the ceremony of the public world; and it is a beautifully wrought and charming scene. The king exhibits a rough-and-ready angular English grace that perfectly delights us as it enchants his lady. But it is not niggling to suggest that, compared with what we have been accustomed to from Prince Hal, now our delight is circumscribed by the extreme self-consciousness and severe modulation of King Henry's rhetoric in wooing:

> Marry, if you would put me to verses or to dance for your sake, Kate, why, you undid me. For the one, I have neither words nor measure; and for the other I have no strength in measure, yet a reasonable measure in strength. If I could win a lady at leapfrog, or by vaulting into my saddle with my armour on my back, under the correction of bragging be it spoken, I should quickly leap into a wife. Or if I might buffet for my love, or bound my horse for her favours, I could lay on like a butcher and sit like a jackanapes, never off. But, before God, Kate, I cannot look greenly nor gasp out my eloquence, nor I have no cunning in protestation; only downright oaths, which I never use till urg'd, nor never break for urging.
>
> (*Henry V*, V.ii.13 ff.)

The bravura eloquence of that speech is, I think, a perfect instance of "ceremony." There is nothing false in it, nothing insincere; it is proof against ironic deflation or parody. But it has nevertheless a certain brittle shaping, the self-conscious modulation of a man whose passions are constantly under the correction of public purposes that by their nature cannot strike deep personal chords. Perhaps the most terrible mortal grief of ceremony is that this prince who once had eloquence enough and an abundance of "cunning in protestation," should now exceed his father's severest expectations in reducing the range of his acquaintance and his rhetoric. Not all of Shakespeare's lovers are so charming as this in their wooing; but none at all are quite so unbending, so effortlessly devoid of passion. Shakespeare's lovers, young and old, are not generally under the cloud of ideological commitment that is central to *Henry V,* and so they win from their experience both deeper pain and greater love than is possible here.

Yet King Henry and his lady do remind us vividly of one couple in Shakespeare—Hotspur and his Kate of the pungent English name:

> Come, wilt thou see me ride?
> And when I am a-horseback, I will swear
> I love thee infinitely. But hark you, Kate;
> I must not have you henceforth question me
> Whither I go, nor reason whereabout.
> Whither I must, I must; and to conclude,
> This evening must I leave you, gentle Kate.
> I know you wise; but yet no farther wise
> Than Harry Percy's wife; constant you are,
> But yet a woman; and for secrecy,
> No lady closer, for I well believe
> Thou wilt not utter what thou dost not know,
> And so far will I trust thee, gentle Kate.
>   (*I Henry IV*, II.iii.103-15)

Hotspur's intonation is more supple and relaxed than the king's. He has known his lady longer, and he enjoys no great office to whose image he must attend. But there is the same bravura movement in his style as in King Henry's; and behind this is a striking similarity in personal range between the warrior king of this play and that early rival whom he canceled out now to supplant. "I know not why *Shakespeare* now gives the king nearly such a character as he made him formerly ridicule in *Percy*," says Dr. Johnson;[7] throughout *Henry V* the king's stiff articulation and ceremonial conduct belie those claims to a supple, "modern" democratic education made by Prince Hal in *Henry IV;* and the simple resounding charm of his style echoes repeatedly the heavy Coriolan clanging of Hotspur's rather than the complex, humane intelligence of Falstaff's and Prince Hal's. I should venture a step beyond Dr. Johnson and suggest that Shakespeare did not set out to give the king such a character as he formerly ridiculed in Percy, but that he discovered by the high art of his play that this is after all a very likely character for the king who salvages degree and thereby saves his country. It needs to be re-emphasized that there is nothing mean or low in that brightly burnished character; it is only vastly diminished in humanity from Prince Hal's; and that diminution, Shakespeare concludes, is a necessary price for the defense of the kingdom. To celebrate the ideal of order as an ultimate political value is to step backward from Prince Hal's "modernity" toward the circumscribed world of Hotspur's rhetoric and personality. And once Shakespeare makes this key discovery, he must reconstitute his faith in the traditional doctrine of order.

An American must be diffident in making so strong a claim, for one may easily mistake the tone of a national rhetoric not one's own. The particular style of a people's devotion to its history is often impenetrable to others; and surely *Henry V* strikes chords in English hearts that do not vibrate in ours. In one sense we may not quarrel with the following remarks of Arthur Sewell:

> It is easy to reduce Shakespeare's treatment of kingship to the prose of politics, and many critics have done so. But there is one problem in Shakespeare's representation of kings which is not susceptible of this kind of treatment, for it is the indisputable work of poetry and has nothing to do with prose. This is his portrayal of royalty. Richard II is royal, even though as man he forfeits his right to be king. . . . Royalty has its unmistakable style and reveals itself as certainly as greatness of soul in a work of art. It is the style in which a particular address to the world, a royal address, is transformed into poetry, and I dare say, unmistakable as it is, and absolutely unmistakable in Henry V, it defies analysis. . . . For Shakespeare political order was something more than temporal, and was not to be explained in the handbook. There was a mystical element in it, which not prose but only poetry could represent, and a part of this element is royalty.[8]

But it is still possible to question whether royalty's address to the world, as formulated in these plays, is capable of being transformed into Shakespeare's greatest poetry even at this stage of his development. It is possible to speak also of the poetry of Falstaff's prose, which renders an address to the world that balances and limits the address of royalty. Not every meaning susceptible to great poetry is just as inclusive as every other; and we may remind ourselves that Shakespeare's fullest rendition of royalty was to come in King Lear's descent from self-dramatization into madness. One need not deny its mystical character in order to suggest that royalty is not presented as a supreme human value even in the Henriad, where an achievement equally important is Shakespeare's discovery, through the poetry of politics and not its prose, that beyond royalty as rendered here man must find a larger address to the world because this royalty excludes too much that is too dearly human. Shakespeare went on to write greater political plays than these, plays with more compelling mystical elements, and plays that dramatize an address to the world more comprehensive than this one. If we are willing to see the history plays as part of a continuing development and not as a final testament, then we cannot rest content even with the great power with which they render the prose of politics into poetry. We must go on to ask what poetry, and we must answer that it is a kind of poetry that the whole momentum of Shakespeare's development impelled him to surpass.

IV

Most of the plays between *Henry V* (1599) and *Othello* (1604) are the "problem" plays of Shakespeare's middle period. They are variously divided in conception and bitter in tone. Shakespeare is preoccupied with the severing of honor and love, justice and truth, language and reality; and frequently his art can barely articulate his vision of these terrifying discrepancies. In themselves and in relation to each other, these plays constitute an intellectual crisis through which Shakespeare passed on his way to the ripened knowledge of his mature tragedies and his last plays. I believe that a principal element in this crisis was the discovery I have outlined of the human and hence philosophic limitations of the traditional doctrines of order, correspondence, and degree.

A speech from one of these plays, Ulysses' address on "the specialty of rule" in *Troilus and Cressida,* is the evidence customarily adduced for Shakespeare's permanent adherence to the traditional doctrines. But it is characteristic of Shakespeare's art that he should bring these doctrines forward from the implicit background of his material and give them inflated expression by a garrulous character only when he has stopped believing in them as given and wishes instead to present them experimentally as a debatable alternative. And *Troilus and Cressida* itself offers eloquent testimony to their problematic character as a criterion of human life. It is not *Troilus and Cressida,* however, but *Julius Caesar* that I now want to discuss briefly as a symptom of Shakespeare's crisis. *Julius Caesar* is a play evidently of the same year as *Henry V* and just as political in its concerns. With the possible exception of *Hamlet* it is the most intensely political play Shakespeare was to write between the Henriad and the key play of his entire development, *King Lear,* to which I will turn in the next chapter. And of course, in its historical material *Julius Caesar* is a preface to *Antony and Cleopatra.*

The play can be cogently interpreted, with appropriate documentation from sixteenth-century political theory, in either one of two contradictory ways: as a catechism on the inevitable evil resulting from political rebellion under any circumstances, or on the evil of an arbitrary political tyranny that justifies rebellion in order to preserve the commonwealth.[9] The former interpretation is proposed by Antony, in his speech over the warm corpse of Caesar at the Capitol and in his funeral oration; and Antony helps justify this interpretation by making his own Machiavellian contribution to the civil disorder that follows the assassination. Brutus proposes the latter interpretation, in his orchard soliloquy and his funeral oration; and much of Caesar's conduct while alive justifies Brutus' conclusions. But of course, Shakespeare cannot have it both ways and still achieve a coherent resolution of the play's dramatic conflict; and his continual juggling of the two interpretations shows him irresolute in his attitude toward that very doctrine which almost simultaneously he had written *Henry V* in order to vindicate.

Whether he is regarded as the actual or merely the titular hero of the play, Caesar himself is surely the subject of Shakespeare's irresolution. And the most conspicuous thing about Caesar is that, like Richard II, he keeps claiming a supernatural status even while exhibiting his human frailty. He claims to be fearless, resolute, impregnable to flattery, superstition, or prejudice, and concerned with the state's welfare before his own. We discover him to be a mediocre swimmer, almost deaf in one ear, fearful, irresolute in the face of flattery and superstition, and concerned with his own welfare before the state's. This discrepancy is illustrated early in the play out of his own mouth, in his warning to Antony to beware of lean men like Cassius,

> I rather tell thee what is to be fear'd
> Than what I fear; for always I am Caesar.
> Come on my right hand, for this ear is deaf,
> And tell me truly what thou think'st of him.
>
> (I.ii.211–14)

and in the last speech of his life, which earns his assassination. Having changed his mind twice about coming to the Capitol on the fateful Ides of March; having been persuaded finally by the prospect of being crowned emperor; and having lied away his safety in his rebuke to Artimedorus, "Who touches us ourself shall be last served," (the only time in the play when Caesar uses the royal "we") ; in a final grandiose gesture he disjoins remorse from power and claims the virtue of *constancy* in rejecting the conspirators' plea to enfranchise Publius Cimber.

> I could be well mov'd, if I were as you;
> If I could pray to move, prayers would move me:
> But I am constant as the Northern Star,
> Of whose true-fix'd and resting quality
> There is no fellow in the firmament.
> The skies are painted with unnumb'red sparks,

They are all fire, and every one doth shine;
But there's but one in all doth hold his place.
So in the world: 'Tis furnish'd well with men,
And men are flesh and blood, and apprehensive;
Yet in the number I do know but one
That unassailable holds on his rank,
Unshak'd of motion; and that I am he,
Let me a little show it, even in this—
That I was constant Cimber should be banish'd
And constant do remain to keep him so.

(III.i.58–73)

Here is the same self-dramatization that we have seen in the English heroes, the same clouded claim to be living up to a high ideal. But the conspirators' grievance is not that Caesar has failed to earn this image of himself. It is that he has created a false image in the first place. For young Pompey, in *Antony and Cleopatra,* it is merely a rhetorical question why Cassius and Brutus acted as they did, "but that they would/ Have one man but a man?" (II.vi.18–19). That is the precise justification which Brutus and Cassius claimed. That Pompey should repeat it exactly, many years and many plays later, suggests how important to Shakespeare was the idea of Caesar's self-dramatization. But now the content of that self-dramatization is secularized, so to speak. The "Caesar-idea" is the character's own invention, not a familiar established doctrine like that of order and degree.[10] Although the qualities that Caesar falsely claims for himself are admirable in a political leader, in this play they are conspicuously not conceived as intrinsic to his vocation or his place in the structure of the world. Whereas Richard and Prince Hal fail to live up to a divine status in which all the characters believe, Caesar is murdered simply for projecting any such image of himself.

Hence Caesar's conduct arouses an antagonist who is able to oppose him only through the medium of a similar self-dramatization. Brutus' delusions of infallibility are as grandiose as those of Richard or Caesar. Although he is one of those notable Shakespearean heroes who seldom know themselves, he above all is supremely confident that he understands other men. He joins the conspiracy because of what he thinks Caesar will become; once he has joined, he continually overrides Cassius in persuading the others not to enlist Cicero, not to take an oath, to let Antony live, and to let him speak at the funeral. Shakespeare represents Brutus' blind will in these matters independently of the outcome of the conspiracy. Brutus' judgment of Antony is mistaken and eventually ruins his cause. But his exclusion of Cicero and his rejection of an oath show the same unbending egotism, though they do not affect the outcome. Brutus' fault is not his misjudgment of Antony but his refusal to test in the tribunal of conspirators either his judgment of Antony or anything else, his refusal to entertain even the possibility that his judgment is mistaken. His confidence is frozen by his need to think properly of himself as the descendant of that other Brutus who drove the Tarquin out of Rome; and this frenetic confidence makes him impregnable to correction on the occasions when he does miscalculate.

After the failure of the conspiracy, Brutus resorts to increasingly ceremonious gestures in order to salvage his image of himself. In the quarrel scene at Sardis he scolds Cassius for taking bribes, and then for refusing to give him some of the money raised, since he himself "can raise no money by vile means." In the much-debated episode of the duplicate revelation of Portia's death, when Messala informs him of what he already knows, Brutus pretends not to have heard it before, so that he can give Messala and Cassius a high-sounding demonstration of Stoic piety. And on the battlefield at Philippi, he compulsively invokes his good name in a piece of witless incantation:

> And I am Brutus, Marcus Brutus I!
> Brutus, my country's friend! Know me for Brutus!
>
> (V.iv.7–8)

These last speeches are the dramatically logical and humanly probable outcome of Brutus' self-dramatization once the conspiracy has failed; and that itself is a reason, to be added to others frequently adduced, for hesitating to believe that these speeches are instances of textual corruption.[11]

A full description of Brutus' character, as of Caesar's, would have to concern itself with a great deal more than self-dramatization. Such a one-sided account as I have given here is unfairly disparaging to both characters. In Caesar's several manifestations of a fine courage, in Brutus' genuine political idealism, and in both men's relations with their wives, friends, and servants, both are exceptional and heroic men. But in *Julius Caesar* the thickening atmosphere of self-dramatization, with its resulting confusion of motives and goals, becomes increasingly a substitute for the firm underpinning of political doctrine that was prominent in Shakespeare's history plays. In *Julius Caesar*, until Antony's funeral oration, nobody speaks or stands for a coherent conception of political order by which to judge men and events. In ways that I have already described, Rome's stability is assured independently of the characters' efforts to resolve their particular political crisis. The details of that crisis are then kept ambiguous and their interconnections are kept deliberately obscure. The characters are forced to act and react only through their disembodied images of themselves and each other. Caesar's self-dramatization, like Richard's and Prince Hal's, reflects the disjoining of public and private values and, behind that, the problematic character of the public world. But in *Julius Caesar* these public and private discords are no longer susceptible of correction by forces operating on behalf of any principle of order, either the order defined by the traditional doctrine of degree or a Roman republican order instead. There is no dramatic equivalent for Bolingbroke and his reformed son to provide the medium and momentum by which order reasserts itself. The only answer to Caesar's self-dramatization is Brutus'; and this only deepens the existing political confusion. The histrionic posturing that in the structure of the history plays was a subordinate element in the larger framework of the traditional doctrine of order now becomes an independent element which itself determines the structure of *Julius Caesar*.

As soon as we go behind the façade of self-dramatization, we find only incoherent details. To the question of whether Caesar is in fact a tyrant and the rebellion justified, the play gives no dependable answer. Brutus, quite apart from both his self-dramatization and his genuine idealism, gives highly inconsistent reasons for adhering to the conspiracy. In his orchard soliloquy and his funeral oration, he puts the case against Caesar's ambition; he is worried that Caesar might become a tyrant in the indefinite future. But to the conspirators he speaks of "the time's abuse," the "high-sighted tyranny" of the present. He explains to Antony that "pity to the general wrong of Rome . . . Hath done this deed on Caesar"; and at Sardis he reminds Cassius that they had killed Caesar "for supporting robbers." He shifts his ground precisely where his idealistic scrupulosity requires the greatest consistency.

Brutus is opposed by Antony, who further compounds confusion. In Antony, Shakespeare makes a stab at providing in this play an agency comparable to that of Bolingbroke and Henry V in the English plays. Antony is the medium through which the forces of order, such as they are, aspire to vindicate themselves in theory and to reassert themselves in practice. In his immediate response to Caesar's death, Antony makes the standard prophecy of disorder to follow the killing of the king:

> Over thy wounds now do I prophesy
> (Which, like dumb mouths, do ope their ruby lips
> To beg the voice and utterance of my tongue),
> A curse shall light upon the limbs of men;
> Domestic fury and fierce civil strife
> Shall cumber all the parts of Italy;
>
> (III.i.259–64)

And so forth. Later, in his funeral oration, Antony begins by offering cogent and honorable arguments against the conspirators. Brutus in his oration had claimed that Caesar was ambitious, but had offered no evidence beyond the honor of his name in saying so. Antony denies Brutus' premise not on the basis of his personal reputation but on the evidence: Caesar was faithful and just to him; Caesar's ransoms filled the general treasury; Caesar refused the crown three times at the Lupercal. "Was this ambition?", he has good reason to ask.

But where Prince Hal turned the somersault of reformation in order to vindicate the traditional doctrine of order, Antony now gyrates in the opposite direction. He begins cunningly to manipulate the mob to suit his purposes, which prove to be subversive of political order and aimed only at his personal aggrandizement. His defense of Caesar becomes a cynical stratagem to advance his own Machiavellian cause; and the play's originally ambivalent characterization of Caesar as a symbol of order is reinforced by a still more divided portrait of Antony as defender of the realm.

Nothing could be more eloquent testimony to Shakespeare's ambivalence than his giving Antony in his funeral oration the last-minute evidence of Caesar's will, which at such a time only renders more incoherent the play's treatment of the traditional doctrine of order. The will shows selfless Caesar's generosity toward the common people, his loving performance of his high vocation, and belatedly proves unfounded the conspirators' central fear that the ambitious man would scorn the base degrees by which he did ascend. But the will is a more flagrant *deus ex machina* even than Thomas Rymer claimed Desdemona's handkerchief to be. Unlike that handkerchief, of whose place in Iago's scheme the audience has been fully informed, Caesar's will comes as a complete surprise to everybody—to the conspirators and the audience as well as to the mob whom Antony is addressing; and it is not produced until Caesar is dead and we have finished weighing the shifting evidence on which the conspirators justified their cause, when it is too late to revise coherently our judgment of what has happened. The effect of the will is nevertheless to qualify our approbation of Brutus and his colleagues by dragging in at the last minute the play's single concrete justification for the traditional doctrine of order. But even that capricious effect is canceled immediately by our discovery that Antony has introduced the will only to advance a scheme aimed at subverting order rather than upholding it.

In *Julius Caesar,* then, the politics of order become highly ambiguous in their own terms, and also fatally disjoined from the poetry of character. In the play's confusion of motives and ideals, we see an extension of the incipient thematic tendencies of the history plays; we see a further weakening of Shakespeare's faith in the efficacy of order as the ultimate criterion of human life. The politics of self-dramatization replace the politics of order, because order as traditionally conceived is no longer self-regulating, and because the traditional doctrine of order has proved too restrictive of those facets of human character that have needed to be sublimated through self-dramatization. *Julius Caesar,* like the problem plays, is transitional in Shakespeare's development; it does not represent his final attitude toward the doctrine of order, or toward that doctrine's implications as to the relation between public and private values. But it may be taken to represent his point of deepest doubt concerning that doctrine, and hence a key step toward his climactic treatment of it in *King Lear.*

Chapter Four

THE LATER HISTORY OF THE THEME: DISPLACEMENT OF THE IDEAL IN *HAMLET* AND *KING LEAR*

Less a chronicle play than *King Lear, Hamlet* is even more remote than *Lear* in its connections with the history plays and with *Antony and Cleopatra.* But no account of Shakespeare's development can ignore *Hamlet,* either as a great work in its own right or as a play that raises questions that are answered only by *King Lear.* In Shakespeare's development *Hamlet* and the history plays converge upon *King Lear* from different directions; and if we are to be concerned eventually with the relation between *King Lear* and *Antony and Cleopatra,* then it is important to indicate, however briefly, the place of *Hamlet* in Shakespeare's development as I have been tracing it.

The ghost in *Hamlet,* then, is the outgrowth of Caesar's will, the ambiguous dramatic artifact that we must assess rightly in order to keep the issues of the play clearly in focus. Caesar's will, which bears closely upon the problem of political order, a problem common to the history plays as well as to *Julius Caesar,* is introduced at a time and place at which it breaks the continuity of the action and disorients our thought. But in *Hamlet* we are made to confront the ghost before anything has intervened, so the ambiguity of its status becomes a very hinge to the plot. Then, while the ghost's identity as a murdered king keeps before us the problem of order in the state, its ambiguous status as a ghost—sent either from heaven or from hell—serves to universalize the temporal into a cosmic problem of the providential structure of the universe itself. Because of the ghost's identity as Hamlet's father, the question of its origin becomes finally a question of the origin of the doctrine of order; and Hamlet's immediate task, to vindicate order with justice through revenge, constitutes the severest, if most indirect, test of that doctrine that Shakespeare had yet conceived.

Hamlet is not so overtly political as the earlier plays I have discussed or the later *King Lear* and *Macbeth;* here the rottenness in Denmark, even as it spreads, is I think an ancillary issue. In the series of correspondences among the cosmos, the state, and the person, the middle term is minimized in comparison to the earlier plays, and the emphasis falls upon the relationship between the other two, particularly upon Hamlet's inner conflict in attempting to discover and then discharge his cosmic duty. In its temporal dimension, that duty is the one which Prince Hal had successfully performed with a severe diminution of his capacity for life, and the one which Antony in *Julius Caesar* had stabbed at uncertainly. Hamlet's duty is to purge and heal the rottenness in Denmark caused by the killing of the king. (Despite Claudius' suave efficiency as a political administrator, Shakespeare makes it increasingly clear in the latter part of the play that the crown sits uneasily upon his head, irrespective of Hamlet's knowledge of his crime.) Hamlet's role as private avenger entails the restoration of order and unity in the commonwealth, and hence the fusion of private and public values. But the fact that this role is enjoined by a ghost who proves to be heaven-sent transforms the temporal duty into a cosmic one and shifts the play's center of interest to Hamlet's inner questioning of that duty as it affects both his relationship to his immediate environment and to life itself.[1]

If we consider not Hamlet's character but Hamlet as a character called to a strenuous and frightening task, we must recognize that he impulsively tries out different strategies, like Antony moving back and forth between Rome and Egypt, and that this improvisation is itself an organic part of his response. Among his many behaviors is that histrionic self-dramatization, a self-conscious overstatement verging upon self-deception, which is one of the several qualities that link him with Richard and Prince Hal and Brutus. We can see it in his first response to the ghost's admonition, "Remember me," in his relations with Ophelia and his mother, and in his several comparisons of himself with Fortinbras. But this self-consciousness is never elaborate enough to build up a single false and frozen image of himself. It is interrupted and qualified by some devastating reflections upon himself and his world that leave no room for the easy comfort of self-dramatization, by moments of mindless passion and cruelty, especially toward Ophelia, that cannot be contained by self-dramatization, and by moments of Falstaffian relish for life that he will not let be stunted by self-dramatization. Hamlet's character arises not from a capacity to live by a consistently evasive image of himself but in the opposite capacity to shift rapidly from one attitude to another in an effort to encompass and absorb the full reality of his experience. And with the diminution in histrionic self-consciousness, there is the beginning of that discontinuity in thought and action that is characteristic of *Antony and Cleopatra.*

In one sense we can say that the self-consciousness that formerly has been prominent in the Shakespearean hero is now spread out over the whole play. The effect of slow motion produced by *Hamlet,* which is often explained wholly by the hero's delay, results I think from Shakespeare's unusually discursive treatment of his materials. The play is not only very long but long-winded, and not only in its treatment of Hamlet. Polonius' twenty-line speech that repeats Laertes' thirty-five lines of advice to Ophelia to keep her distance from Hamlet, the needlessly complicated employment of Rosencrantz and Guildenstern, all the arras-hiding and gallery-walking, and the nearly one hundred lines that it takes Claudius and Laertes to hatch their simple plan for the duel, are examples of that orotund dramatic procedure by which the play seems to hold back from itself, as if frightened by the course it is taking. The same effect is produced by the frequency of Hamlet's soliloquies, by his speeches to the players and to the skull of Yorick, and by the play-within-a-play. For all its rapid changes of locale, its eavesdropping and mousetrapping and violent action, *Hamlet* is enveloped in a self-conscious air of suspended animation; and this troubled air, no less than Hamlet's personal response to his world, gives the play its pervasive atmosphere of death and its morbid interest in sniffing at mortality.

Hamlet, then, is marked by signs of Shakespeare's intellectual crisis; however, I do not think that the play is an artistic failure. In Shakespeare's intellectual development *Hamlet* represents truly a moment of suspension and not of paralysis; and within that suspension the artistic center holds. This is not the place to illustrate in detail the artistic integrity of *Hamlet,* but one particular example of it will also suggest *Hamlet*'s connection with the earlier plays I discussed, as well as with *King Lear.* It has often been remarked that Hamlet, unable to carry out his revenge, is set in sharp relief by Fortinbras and Laertes, both of whom are prompt to avenge their fathers. Now Fortinbras and Laertes, like Prince Hal's foils, Hotspur and Falstaff, do not merely duplicate each other; rather, they illustrate two opposite ways of being wrong in the same cause. Laertes, for all his French education, is a true slave of passion: he is ready to cut his enemy's throat in the church without bothering to find out who his enemy rightly is, or whether in fact he has one. Fortinbras, of whom Hamlet says that he will "find quarrel in a straw/ When honour's at the stake," is easily deflected from avenging his father's death by a fight with the Polacks over a piece of land too small to hold the corpses of those who are to die in battle. Laertes is too concerned with his father to remember his honor; Fortinbras is too concerned with his honor to remember his father; therefore they both must dream up specious causes and enemies to suit their needs. They constitute the connected poles between which Hamlet's true cause is circumscribed and defined in all its frightening complexity, and the contrast between them provides a coherent artistic context that remains stable no matter how or whether Hamlet succeeds in finding the right way to serve that filial cause which both of them have wronged.

But it is true, nevertheless, that at the very center of things Hamlet—and behind him Shakespeare—cannot find his way, or at best can only stumble upon it inadvertently at the last minute. Placed between Fortinbras and Laertes, whose roads he knows must not be taken, Hamlet only boggles. No matter how precisely he thinks upon the event, he cannot ascertain what is the right thing to do. But with the careers of Fortinbras and Laertes unfolding before us, we can only honor Hamlet for trying to understand precisely where his duty lies. *Hamlet*, says D. G. James, "is a tragedy not of excessive thought but of defeated thought." [2] For Hamlet, unlike Laertes and Fortinbras, the means must justify the ends; and, in view of the ghost's status and injunctions, the ends themselves must be freshly questioned and validated. It is characteristic of Hamlet's temperament that he should devote himself primarily to this latter task, to finding some ethical, and eventually metaphysical, sanction for revenge that will also sanction his means. Meanwhile, however, he improves the time with whatever means suggest themselves: he puts on his antic disposition, turns away from Ophelia, baits and springs the mousetrap, stabs at the arras, unseals the letters of commission, boards the pirate ship alone, and acts with bloody decisiveness in the duel scene. In all this bustling activity he surely does not delay in taking arms against his troubles. But these various actions are unrelated to each other, or to any coherent plan directed to a particular end; some are premature, and several are in themselves foul means that must taint whatever end they might half-wittingly accomplish. Instead of avoiding the false means of Laertes and Fortinbras, Hamlet thoughtlessly tries first one and then the other. After the players' scene has certified the ghost, he declares himself ready to "drink hot blood/ And do such bitter business as the day/ Would quake to look on." Instead he spares Claudius at prayer in order to go tilt with Polacks in his mother's bedroom. But once there, on the spur of a moment he stabs through the arras without really caring who is on the other side.

Hamlet needs to improvise his disconnected and eventually damning means because, for all his incitement, he is not certain what his troubles are, or whether in fact he ought to take arms against them. He cannot decide upon his immediate ends because he cannot decide upon the ends of human life itself. This brings us to the pivotal speech in which we see his thought defeated, the "To be or not to be" soliloquy. This speech is not concerned simply and exclusively with suicide. The reasons given why men sheer off from suicide are the very same reasons why "enterprises of great pith and moment/ With this regard their currents turn awry." One such additional enterprise for Hamlet must be avenging his murdered father. The question whether one is "To be or not to be" is more than a question whether to remain physically alive amidst the world's stale uses or to kill oneself. That is one possible pair of alternatives. But the whole speech implies that it is possible to be physically alive and still "not to be"; so Hamlet's question is also one of true and false being. Dr. Johnson and D. G. James argue that Hamlet's "To be" refers to eternal life as against temporal life; I am inclined to agree in this instance with G. Wilson Knight's more secular emphasis when he says that Hamlet's "To be" means "not merely to live, to act, but really *to be*." [3] But in either view, Hamlet's fundamental question is *how* we should *live* in order that we may really *be*. The ontological question is inseparable from the ethical question; the issue is not simply whether to face the vicissitudes of life but how to encounter them.

In Hamlet's very next lines the pair of alternatives for being is followed by a pair of alternatives for conduct; and the syntactical parallelism of the two pairs suggests that at least for this moment, Hamlet, and Shakespeare, are defining "to be" as "to suffer the slings and arrows of outrageous Fortune," and are defining "not to be" as "to take arms against a sea of troubles/ And by opposing end them." Now, this parallelism is not elaborated with any consistency either in the remainder of the soliloquy, where Hamlet goes on to wonder whether he should even live, let alone *be,* or in the immediately ensuing action of the play, as Hamlet whirls through his improvised efforts to take arms against his troubles. But after all his disconnected efforts have proved fruitless and Hamlet has come home from England spent, he makes a speech that I think reinstates in the play the opening idea of the soliloquy and makes it the basis for the climactic action of the duel scene. Hamlet has engaged himself for the duel, but then has confessed to Horatio a premonition of disaster. When Horatio offers to call off the duel, Hamlet replies:

> Not a whit, we defy augury; there's a special providence in the fall of a sparrow. If it be now, 'tis not to come; if it be not to come, it will be now; if it be not now, yet it will come: the readiness is all. Since no man knows aught of what he leaves, what is't to leave betimes? Let be.   (V.ii.230 ff.)

In the soliloquy Hamlet looked unsuccessfully for a way to be unafraid of life. Here he finds a way to be unafraid of death, and he sums it up in the words "Let be." Those words appear in the second Quarto but not the Folio; and the Quarto reading, which has been adopted by modern editors, may be taken seriously here because its meaning is integral with the rest of the speech. To be sure, Hamlet is telling Horatio to let the arrangement stand and not to call off the duel. But his "Let be" also implies the definition of "To be" given in the opening lines of the soliloquy: "To be" is indeed to suffer the slings and arrows of fortune, because at the heart of life there is special providence that outmasters Fortune, a divinity rather than a turning wheel that shapes our ends. In the face of that special providence, right conduct requires us to be in a poised state of readiness for death whenever and in whatever form life brings it to us, to keep in continual practice with the sword but not to go stabbing at arrases. Therefore, let the duel be, since that is what life now brings as the providential form in which death, perhaps, will come. Thus, to fight the duel without regard to auguries of Fortune is to participate in true being.

Hamlet is speaking to Horatio, whom he has praised "As one in suff'ring all that suffers nothing": instead of taking arms against Fortune, Horatio has accepted her "buffets and rewards . . . with equal thanks." Now Hamlet proposes to do that same thing and at last becomes eligible to accomplish the revenge. In the last part of *Hamlet,* when the players' scene and the killing of Polonius have transferred the initiative to Claudius, two new elements emerge with vivid force. One is that Hamlet displays a more stable and self-contained attitude than we have seen in him before: his behavior exhibits increasingly (though not uninterruptedly) that forbearance and passivity that he elucidates in the "readiness is all" speech. The other is that Claudius, although his smoothly functioning strategy in meeting the Norwegian threat has led us to expect that his designs against Hamlet will be equally successful, is hoist with his own petard and with him Laertes, who confesses, "I am justly killed by mine own treachery." These two elements are inextricably connected: Hamlet, by virtue of his decision to suffer Fortune's blows and still stand ready for life and death as they come, like Edgar in *King Lear,* becomes the instrument by which evil is returned upon its inventors' heads. Providence proves capable not only of catching up with a slippery character like Claudius but of converting Hamlet, after all his impetuous activity, into the willingly passive instrument necessary to its purpose.

The "readiness is all" speech, and the conduct it belatedly causes, serve to revive the idea suggested momentarily by the soliloquy. But as I have indicated, the "readiness is all" speech is not central in the play. The attitude toward life that it recommends has been exemplified in conduct only by Horatio, a bystander, and not by any character directly involved in the unfolding events. All the central characters, and not just Hamlet, have devoted themselves to taking arms against real or imagined troubles. The idea of the speech has had no precedent in action; the relationship with the soliloquy that I have claimed for it has not been made good in the structure of the play. The speech seems almost to have been inserted as a prop, to relieve for a moment the general pallor of death, and to impart some thematic dignity to the mass bloodshed of the final scene. But the speech voices another conception of the conduct of life than we have seen in the earlier plays I have discussed; it breaks fresh intellectual ground, even if that ground is not the center of action. That is why I think it proper to say that Shakespeare, in writing *Hamlet,* has reached in his development a stage of crisis but not paralysis. He has made a philosophical advance that has not been dramatically consolidated.

In *King Lear* the central idea of Hamlet's "readiness is all" speech is restated in more concentrated form in Edgar's words to his father when Gloucester, with better reason than Hamlet, contemplates suicide:

> What, in ill thoughts again? Men must endure
> Their going hence, even as their coming hither;
> Ripeness is all. Come on.   (V.ii.9–11)

But in *King Lear* the speech does not lie askew of the play's center as in *Hamlet;* instead it voices almost the whole meaning of the action. The good characters of the play—Cordelia, Kent, and Edgar—have lived by its precept, and have thereby made possible the purgation, contrition, and exaltation of Lear, and through Lear, of human life. This speech is made not by an admirer but by Edgar himself, who in suffering all has suffered nothing, and who thereby may emerge as the providential destroyer of evil in the deliberate glory of shining armor rather than the unwitting secrecy of a poisoned sword. Edgar's thought, moreover, has been prefigured elsewhere in the play, as a running thread in its intellectual texture; for example, in Lear's remark to Gloucester, "Thou must be patient; we came crying hither." In a word, the philosophic advance made haltingly in *Hamlet* becomes the basis of *King Lear*'s intellectual and emotional power as Shakespeare's greatest play and the fulcrum of his development. This fact gives Hamlet's "readiness is all" speech a retrospective importance far greater than is warranted by its immediate context.

But to look backward for a moment: in the plays before *Hamlet,* Shakespeare was fundamentally concerned with the problem of political order, which led inevitably to a concern with the relation between character and society in the maintenance of order. He began with a ready-made criterion, an official doctrine of order, with which to explore those relationships, and came increasingly to question the adequacy of his criterion. He discovered by his art the restriction and waste of human vitality, through "ceremony" and self-dramatization, indigenous to a society governed by the doctrine; he was led to imagine, in *Julius Caesar,* a situation in which it becomes questionable whether society can be governed in any case by a doctrine whose precise relevance to the immediate circumstances keeps shifting. In the English plays the order of society was problematic, but the doctrine of order was not; in *Julius Caesar,* the doctrine itself becomes problematic, and *Hamlet* inherits the problem. At this point, necessarily, Shakespeare's center of attention shifts from political order to cosmic order, to the metaphysical sanctions for a temporal doctrine that has come into question. Revenge, unlike rebellion, is concerned directly and immediately with the providential structure of the universe, the cosmic order that allegedly supports the temporal order. In *Hamlet,* the standard doctrine of temporal order just manages to survive this test. There turns out to be a divinity that shapes our ends, certifying the ghost, returning evil upon its authors, and restoring health to the rotted state by providential means beyond man's power to direct and despite his efforts to oppose. But in thus vindicating indirectly the doctrine of order, *Hamlet* does not fully resolve the related problem of conduct, the relation of public to private values, which has been at issue all along. On the one hand, Hamlet is not given to the elaborate posturing of Richard and Prince Hal and Brutus because he is confronting the ethical questions that their histrionics are designed to evade. On the other hand, he cannot achieve the impassivity of Horatio soon enough to make it count because he does not find in time a proper answer to his double-barrelel question, "To be or not to be." In the gallery of Shakespeare's heroes, Hamlet wanders back and forth between two types, one not quite dead, the other still unborn; and that is one reason for his fascination as a character. I think it is also one reason why the play is soaked in an atmosphere of death that frequently emanates from Hamlet himself. Unable either to evade his problem by self-dramatization or to resolve it by forbearance, often Hamlet has nothing to do but rail against the world and its uses, in that *de contemptu* imagery of sickness and rot which has often been remarked.[4] And Hamlet's revulsion from life, in its philosophic bent if not its tone of nausea, anticipates Lear's final wish to be released from the uses of this world and to look down from his comfortably walled prison upon the human comedy as a spy from God.

II

I have made much of the word *be* in *Hamlet;* and the importance of *nothing* in *King Lear* is well known. It is not too much to say that these two plays constitute Shakespeare's essay on being and nothingness in both the Augustinian and Sartrian meanings of those words. In *King Lear* Shakespeare completes his long negotiation with the doctrine of order that he inherited from his culture. He finally affirms that doctrine with great conviction, but with a sharply curtailed faith in its scope and importance. In the history plays he had explored the human cost of preserving order, and the discrepancy between public and private values, in a world whose ultimate value was order itself. In *Julius Caesar* he had questioned whether order can be maintained as a coherent value, either ultimate or proximate, without regard to cost. *King Lear* answers that question affirmatively, but only by denying that order can be a final value. In the earlier plays order was sought (in the very different ways of Prince Hal, Henry V, Brutus, and Mark Antony) by taking arms against disorder and thereby fragmenting human character by wrenching apart public and private values. In *King Lear* Shakespeare links the doctrine of order to the doctrine of conduct that he had explored in *Hamlet*: now at last order is guaranteed by those like Cordelia, Kent, and Edgar, for whom there is no gap between public and private values, and hence no self-dramatization, because they are able to suffer the slings and arrows of fortune on behalf of the traditional principle of order. But this act of forbearance is seen finally as a means and not an end, as a minimum condition of life that preserves us from chaos and dissolution but is not in itself the fulfilment of our humanity. On the one hand, *King Lear* confirms what *Hamlet* had anticipated and proves the doctrine of order in the most convincing way possible: it shows a world with an almost unlimited capacity for evil and disorder, providentially brought to rights by those who live according to the traditional doctrine of order. On the other hand, that proof implies an acceptance of the world's enormous potentiality for disorder, a recognition that the problematics of the social order are a permanent condition of life. *King Lear* does not reveal conditions under which social order may become immutable and universal peace be guaranteed indefinitely; the play assures us only that when society falls apart, as it is bound to do from time to time, certain constructive forces of Nature are equally bound to come forward and restore it. Once Shakespeare has earned this assurance by the insight achieved through his art, the problem of order is over for him, and the question arises: Where does life go from here? For the highest powers of human life are not exhausted in the bare maintenance of a social order that contains within it, necessarily, a cyclic potentiality for disruption. In his effort to discover the life beyond politics that yet cannot be free of politics, Shakespeare went on to write *Antony and Cleopatra* and his last plays, which are no less serious than *King Lear*. We must now begin to trace this progression.

None of Shakespeare's tragedies more wholly contains its end in its beginning than *King Lear*; and in the beginning is Lear's self-dramatization. It is often argued that Lear's original mistake, and the source of all his woe, is resigning the kingship and dividing the kingdom among his daughters. According to the traditional doctrine of order, this abrogation is an offense against both divine and natural law from which only chaos can result; and in that respect, *King Lear* certainly bears out the doctrine. But I do not think Shakespeare is performing anything like so mechanical and limited a demonstration of the doctrine at this stage of his maturity. Lear has made his decision to abdicate before the play begins, and in the first scene he proposes to divide the kingdom in a public ceremony whose express purpose is "that future strife/ May be prevented now" and the peaceful continuity of political order be assured. The first scene goes on to demonstrate, with an unparalleled rigor and amplitude of evidence, that Lear's mistake lies not in the wish of an eighty-year old man to resign the burden of kingship but in the histrionic means he chooses to execute his purpose, the speech-making contest that leads inexorably to the rejection of those who truly love him, Cordelia and Kent. This rejection, and not the division of the kingdom, is the mainspring of the action; and it is here that Shakespeare comes to grips with the doctrine of order.

The nature of Lear's mistake, from which momentous consequences are to follow, is worth being precise about, and, at the risk of seeming to quibble, I must press this argument. It would be wholly uncharacteristic of Shakespeare to allow his protagonist to commit the tragic error offstage before the play begins. Moreover, even if he were so awkwardly obscure, he would not muddy the waters further by devoting the play's first scene to the protagonist's second mistake and making it the single cause of universal disapprobation by an eloquent group of choric characters, including the villains of the play. Before the first scene has ended, Cordelia, Kent, France, Goneril, and Regan—fully half the number of people on the stage besides Lear himself—have separately called our attention to Lear's folly in judging his daughters by their speeches and therefore rejecting Cordelia and Kent. But nobody has said a critical word about Lear's decision to resign the throne and divide the kingdom. Kent, who is now ready to risk his life in order to convince Lear that he has misjudged Cordelia, originally had the opportunity to confess privately to Gloucester, without risking Lear's displeasure, whatever misgivings he might have had over Lear's decision to divide the kingdom. Instead, he only voiced surprise that in the division Lear did not favor Albany over Cornwall, a favoritism that, according to standard doctrine, would have compounded the evil of dividing the kingdom in the first place. Shakespeare's whole procedure in the first scene not only ignores but implicitly rejects the possibility that Lear's mistake was the division of the kingdom.

Instead, it is Lear's self-dramatization, first in his anticipation of flattering speeches from his daughters, and then in his response to Cordelia's refusal to gratify him, that causes both the disruption of the state and Lear's personal suffering. In order to soften the stark reality of his final surrender of political power, Lear misappropriates that power to private ends and misuses it to force upon his daughters a false test of filial piety. Once his mistake is exposed by Cordelia's refusal to humor him, he retreats further and further into a false image of himself as wronged omnipotence, like Richard and Prince Hal and Brutus and Caesar under comparable pressures. This is reflected in the vehemence with which he disowns Cordelia, and then in the banishment of Kent:

> Hear me, recreant!
> On thine allegiance, hear me!
> Since thou hast sought to make us break our vow—
> Which we durst never yet—and with strain'd pride
> To come between our sentence and our power,—
> Which nor our nature nor our place can bear,—
> Our potency made good, take thy reward.
> Five days we do allot thee for provision
> To shield thee from diseases of the world,
> And on the sixth to turn thy hated back
> Upon our kingdom. If, on the tenth day following,
> Thy banish'd trunk be found in our dominions,
> The moment is thy death. Away! By Jupiter,
> This shall not be revok'd.   (I.i.169–82)

Clearly, the "strain'd pride" is Lear's, since the kingdom is no longer his to defend, and since the arbitrary power he invokes on the flimsiest pretext was not rightfully his even when the kingdom was. But on the ceremonial occasion of surrending his power, Lear needs desperately to assert his authority, to invoke the image of a king without the humane judgment that befits the conduct of a king. And just as the disowning of Cordelia led to the banishment of Kent, so now Lear becomes entangled in his image of himself as the play unfolds, and increasingly loses touch with the actual circumstances of his life, until the storm and his madness come to purge him.

At the end of the first scene, Shakespeare makes Lear's self-dramatization an excuse for his evil daughters' harshness; ironically, they use "the infirmity of his age" and Lear's "unruly waywardness" as reasons for turning against him. Lear continues to exhibit these qualities by his distracted behavior in Goneril's household; for example, he capriciously engages the disguised Kent in a single speech—"If I like thee no worse after dinner, I will not part from thee yet"—and then goes on to call for his dinner and his fool with childish impatience. If we had not heard Goneril's and Kent's original warnings against her, and if we had not seen Goneril instruct Oswald to insult her father, we could almost side with Goneril when she confronts Lear.

Lear.   Are you our daughter?

Gon.   Come, sir,
    I would you would make use of that good wisdom
    Whereof I know you are fraught, and put away
    These dispositions that of late transform you
    From what you rightly are.

Fool.   May not an ass know when the cart draws the horse?
    Whoop, Jug, I love thee!

Lear.   Doth any here know me? This is not Lear.
    Doth Lear walk thus? speak thus? Where are his eyes?
    Either his notion weakens, his discernings
    Are lethargied—Ha! waking? 'Tis not so!
    Who is it that can tell me who I am?

Fool.   Lear's shadow.

Lear.   I would learn that; for, by the marks of sovereignty,
    Knowledge, and reason, I should be false persuaded
    I had daughters.

Fool.   Which they will make an obedient father.

Lear.   Your name, fair gentlewoman?

Gon.   This admiration, sir, is much o' th' savour
    Of other your new pranks. I do beseech you
    To understand my purposes aright.
    As you are old and reverend, you should be wise.

                                        (I.iv.238–61)

Later the Fool is to echo Goneril and tell Lear he should not have been old before he became wise. Goneril is entirely accurate in identifying Lear's histrionic behavior, and in calling his "admiration" that image of himself by which he must now live, since he has relied upon it in cutting himself off from both his public office and his only loving daughter.

In the history plays self-dramatization was a symptom of public disorder, an unstable reflection through the protagonist's image of himself of some prior maladjustment in his society. Then, in the ambiguous treatment of his materials in *Julius Caesar,* Shakespeare anticipated the reversal of the relationship between public and private elements that now emerges in *King Lear,* where the protagonist's self-dramatization, instead of reflecting social disorder, constitutes that very rebellion which produces disruption in the family, the state, and the world. I have stressed the nature of Lear's tragic error partly to indicate the relationship between his histrionics and those of his predecessors, but mostly because of the importance in Shakespeare's development of this reversal in the relationship between social disorder and self-dramatization, a reversal that destroys the earlier monolithic emphasis on public order as the supreme value in human life. The old emphasis had earlier been undermined by the insistence in *Julius Caesar* upon Rome's indestructibility despite the intrigues of the characters, and by the focus of *Hamlet* upon the question of private conduct. Now in *King Lear,* making the hero's conduct a cause and not a reflection of public disorder serves to transfer the weight of Shakespeare's emphasis from politics to ethics. At the same time, Shakespeare does not minimize the problem of order and make it ancillary to the problem of conduct, as in *Hamlet* and *Othello.* His protagonist is the king himself, whose personal conduct is the immediate source and warrant for public order. But in basing the play's action on Lear's rebellion through self-dramatization, and in making Lear's histrionic behavior sympathetically appealing in a man of his age and temperament, Shakespeare sees that public order cannot remain indefinitely stable when part of the wonder (and misery) of life lies in the unpredictable desires of which private men are capable. According to the standard doctrine, Lear's mistake is gratuitous. It is not a political offense like tyranny, playing favorites, or unfair taxation; it does not directly impair the king's function in the commonwealth. It simply undermines the theory by which that royal function is authorized. It is such an act of self-indulgence as any citizen might commit to set off his tragedy. Thus Shakespeare recognizes that personal ethics, whose vulnerability is the permanent source of tragedy, must nevertheless be the permanent source and measure of political order. Order, then, is endlessly subject to tragic dissolution; and this fact, while it excludes the history plays' compulsive concern for the permanence of order, does not diminish but enhances the human importance of the problem of order. By subordinating it to the problem of conduct, Shakespeare transforms the problem of order from a subject for chronicle plays to a subject for tragedy.

The precise manner in which Lear's self-dramatization affronts the doctrine of order is indicated, not surprisingly, by his use of the word "nature" on two occasions during the opening scene. In proposing the speechmaking contest, he asks his daughters,

> Which of you shall we say doth love us most?
> That we our largest bounty may extend
> Where nature doth with merit challenge.   (I.i.52–54)

And in the speech already quoted in which he banishes Kent, he says,

> Since thou hast sought to make us break our vow—
> Which we durst never yet—and with strain'd pride
> To come between our sentence and our power,—
> Which nor our nature nor our place can bear,—
> Our potency made good, take thy reward.

The word has a more general reference in the first passage than in the second; but this difference is unimportant next to the fact that in both cases Lear makes a disjunction between "nature" on the one hand and "merit" or "place" on the other.

In the traditional doctrine these three elements are equivalent: man's human nature is to occupy his cosmic place with merit; his place is merited by his nature; and his merit is his place in nature. To have one of these attributes is to have them all. It is possible, of course, to use the expressions "nature with merit" and "nor our nature nor our place" in a conjunctive sense, in which the two terms in each pair are meant to be synonymous. As the context makes clear, however, that is not what Lear is doing. In asking his daughters for speeches, he makes a fateful disjunction between the nature of children to love their parents and the merit of oratory whose profession of love may not be natural; and then he bets his bounty on the latter. That is why he is doubly surprised when Cordelia refuses to act upon his distinction and insists upon the identity of nature, place, and merit by saying "Nothing." Cordelia's plain adherence to the old doctrine affronts him in the headlong pride of his self-dramatization, and all he can manage to do is trap himself in his false distinction by disowning Cordelia.

Now Lear has opened the door of the kingdom to disruption and domination by those characters who base their ethics on his false distinction. Having disowned Cordelia and her "doctrine of nature," Lear is stuck with his own and that of Edmund.[5] Edmund's soliloquy, which states the rationale for evil in the play, is nothing more than an elaboration of Lear's distinction between nature and merit, which Edmund calls "invention":

> Thou, Nature, art my goddess; to thy law
> My services are bound. Wherefore should I
> Stand in the plague of custom, and permit
> The curiosity of nations to deprive me,
> For that I am some twelve or fourteen moonshines
> Lag of a brother? . . .
>   . . . Well then,
> Legitimate Edgar, I must have your land.
> Our father's love is to the bastard Edmund
> As to th' legitimate. Fine word—'legitimate'!
> Well, my legitimate, if this letter speed,
> And my invention thrive, Edmund the base
> Shall top th' legitimate. I grow; I prosper.
> Now, gods, stand up for bastards!   (I.ii.1–22)

Edmund simply takes the distinction one little step beyond where Lear left it, and in the process his logic is impeccable. Where Cordelia had identified "merit" with "nature," insisting that a person's merit is his proper place and conduct within the whole structure of nature, and where Lear had denied this identification without implying an alternative, now Edmund resolves Lear's disjunction by reversing Cordelia's identification and making "merit" antecedent to "nature." Edmund insists that there is in nature no original structure but only a random distribution of talent and "invention," and that the plague of custom and its rhetoric of legitimacy frustrate our proper efforts to finally achieve the fluidity intended by Nature in her originally fortuitous distribution of talents. Cordelia's nature was a structure in which fixed gradations of place give rise to specific obligations of conduct, which mutually support the structure of the whole. For this Edmund substitutes a nature in which the only gradations are the unpredictable ones of individual wit and fortune and the only obligations are to make invention thrive and to hope for Fortune's blessing. The final aim of conduct is therefore to preserve the enticing indeterminacy of Nature and to prevent her from attaining a fixed structure that limits the bounty of Fortune but happens to be necessary to human mutuality.

Goneril echoes Edmund in the very next scene, where Shakespeare pays this philosophy its due with a profound and terrifying lucidity. Edmund has come bouncing onto the stage in the familiar guise of the Machiavel and has announced his theory to the world at large. Goneril puts the theory into practice on her father, and Shakespeare makes Lear's conduct seem to justify the treatment. In telling Oswald to "Put on what weary negligence you please" toward her father, Goneril says:

> Now, by my life,
> Old fools are babes again, and must be us'd
> With checks as flatteries, when they are seen abus'd.
> (I.iii.18–20)

Goneril's readiness to use Lear is of a piece with Edmund's "invention" aimed at abusing his father. At this point it would have been easy for a lesser dramatist than Shakespeare to show Goneril's criticism of Lear to be groundless, to make her evil seem unprompted and all the more melodramatically monstrous. But Shakespeare now brings Lear on the stage, in that scene of self-dramatization from which I have quoted at length, and makes his childish behavior in hiring Kent and crying for his dinner give credence to Goneril's remark that old fools are babes again. Just as Goneril and Regan at the beginning used Lear's rashness with Cordelia as a reason to harden themselves against him, so now Shakespeare leaves open the possibility that Lear and his knights *have* been so riotous as to disrupt Goneril's household. It is true that Lear and a knight specifically deny that charge, but a great part of Lear's behavior on the stage confirms it. Shakespeare wants it clear that even if Goneril is right about Lear's behavior in her household, she is as wrong now as she was in the opening scene to bargain with him over it. For Goneril as for Edmund, merit is matter for invention, and man must get all he can by his wits, whether in forged speeches, forged letters, or in the use of checks and flatteries.

Or even by physical cruelty. Part of the terror in *King Lear* is aroused because Lear and Gloucester seem to "deserve" the Machiavellian policy wrought upon them by their wicked children. But the greater fright is in the swiftness with which that policy degenerates into an inhuman sadism that far exceeds the requirements of any policy—in the shuttlecock game by which Lear's daughters bounce him back and forth till he is deprived of all his knights, in their turning him out in the storm to lose his wits ("Mine enemy's dog,/ Though he had bit me, should have stood that night/ Against my fire," Cordelia says later), and in the visible blinding of Gloucester. These acts are not necessary pieces of "invention" in the service of Edmund's "Nature"; they do nothing to advance the Machiavellian design of the evil characters. Rather, they show the gratuitous bestiality into which mankind is inevitably betrayed by the pursuit of Machiavellian policy. Such actions lead us overwhelmingly to Lear's question whether discarded fathers should have such little mercy upon their own flesh, and they make his answer our own: ". . . 'twas this flesh begot/ Those pelican daughters."

But there are good children who, the play tells us, redeem Nature from the general curse to which the evil ones have brought her. Over against Edmund and Goneril stand Cordelia and Edgar, who have the patient readiness to endure their parents' wrongs and still not abate their filial love or duty. Cordelia and Edgar willingly enact the traditional doctrine of order, on behalf of which they are ready to suffer the adversities of fortune. Although their gratuitous action provides neither challenge nor counterweight to the control of events by Edmund and his cohorts, nevertheless it eventually serves to draw from the world the poison with which it had been infected both by Lear's original disjunction between nature and merit and by the resulting hegemony of Edmund. Where the policied pursuit of Fortune's blessings by the evil children leads to meaningless cruelty, the steadfast acceptance of Fortune's buffets by the good children leads to meaningful suffering, and thereby lights their parents' way out of Edmund's and Goneril's midnight world. Having to acknowledge of the older children that human flesh can beget such pelicans is the price to be paid for having these children answer for the permanence of love out of which to weave the fabric of human life.

III

Lear's tragic suffering, which was made possible in the first place by Cordelia's truth, carries him eventually from his negotiated place in Goneril's household back into the arms of Cordelia. In Lear's onslaught of madness there is something so apparently unmediated by art that the play has always been painful to witness on the stage, and about such pain it is hard to speak clearly. We must keep before us the character and extent of Lear's transformation, because in the bleak ending of *King Lear* there is no other evidence for the practical efficacy of suffering love in the good children, no other hope for the refreshment of life, than the change we have witnessed in Lear himself. To ignore that change because it is familiar, or to misread its place among other prominent elements in the denouement, is to misapprehend the play's grim outcome.

Lear's chastisement by a storm of nature without and within passes through several distinct stages, and merely the first of these is his recognition, still on this side of madness, of his brotherhood with other men and his former carelessness toward them. Stripped of his knights and denied even shelter in a storm, Lear's first reaction had been to tax the elements for joining with his wicked daughters to hurt a man so old, helpless, and almost innocent. That self-pity, however, was the last layer of Lear's former self-dramatized image of himself. Now, finally, he forgets himself and thinks of others. He makes the Fool precede him into the shelter as a prelude to his speech,

> Poor naked wretches, whereso'er you are,
> That bide the pelting of this pitiless storm,
> How shall your houseless heads and unfed sides,
> Your loop'd and window'd raggedness, defend you
> From seasons such as these? O, I have ta'en
> Too little care of this! Take physic, pomp;
> Expose thyself to feel what wretches feel,
> That thou mayst shake the superflux to them
> And show the heavens more just.   (III.iv.28–36)

But Lear and we are not permitted to rest even in this deep and difficult knowledge; we are only allowed to imagine for the last time that what has gone wrong was merely adventitious and may still be put right by a corrective on the existing scales of justice, with the superflux of one side shifted to the other. But for Shakespeare, Lear's original deed has pushed the world too far out of kilter to be rebalanced so easily. Not only is the specific character of order as defined by traditional doctrine now in question but also the very source and possibility of order in the world. Lear has earned by his error the need to face that question, and therefore he must now go mad. He must descend into the original chaos of Nature out of which the order of justice in society, as well as the order of the human mind itself, must be formed and reformed. It is a descent into nothingness out of which something may yet come; and Lear's ultimate royalty is to make that descent.

Lear next goes through an intermediate stage in the mock trial of Goneril and Regan. In seeking to present evidence in court against them and in all his talk of robed justice, equity, arraignment, and oath-taking, he is appealing to ostensible forms of justice no longer applicable to his experience, and his discovery of the irrelevance carries him fully and finally into madness.

When at last he comes on the stage at Dover wearing his crown of weeds, there is no further descent from sanity—since Lear has now reached bottom—but only the lateral expansion of his encounter with original chaos. He said to Cordelia in the opening scene that nothing would come of her "nothing." But for him now total deprivation has come of it: he has lost his outward royalty, his family, knights, shelter, clothing, and wits; and yet to have lost all that, to have reached the question whether there is any cause in nature for such denudation, is to have come after all, with the precision of a philosopher, from "nothing" to nothing. Lear has passed behind human justice and now reason itself in order to find the status in Nature of this nothing; and it is now to be discovered whether nature will offer a demonic pattern for Regan's hard heart, or a benign warrant for that patience which Lear had prized and lost, or whether Nature, like Cordelia, will answer nothing.

Short of quoting this scene (IV.vi) in full, which is the one way to do justice to its dense mixture of profundity and irrelevance, we can only enumerate the most conspicuous motifs in Lear's raving. Three such elements are inextricably woven together. The first is Lear's continuing ironic affirmation of his royalty even in the midst of his impotence and loss: "No, they cannot touch me for coining; I am the king himself." "Ay, every inch a king :/ When I do stare, see how the subject quakes." "None does offend, none, I say, none; I'll able 'em." "Come come; I am a king, masters, know you that?" He keeps harping upon the absolute potency that he was so jealous to defend against Cordelia and Kent in the beginning. Yet that he can call himself a king and his captors "masters" in a single breath indicates that his royal authority is not autonomous after all, but subject to a dispensation beyond himself. Lear has acknowledged that indirectly in a poignant speech near the beginning of this sequence:

> Ha! Goneril with a white beard? They flatter'd me like a dog, and told me I had white hairs in my beard ere the black ones were there. To say 'ay' and 'no' to everything I said! 'Ay' and 'no' too was no good divinity. When the rain came to wet me once, and the wind to make me chatter; when the thunder would not peace at my bidding; there I found 'em, there I smelt 'em out. Go to, they are not men o' their words! They told me I was everything. 'Tis a lie—I am not ague-proof. (IV.vi.97–107)

Here is the same insistence upon his potency—"there I smelt 'em out"—but coupled with the sharp awareness that neither agues nor thunder will spare him. An intense pathos arises from our awareness, over and beyond Lear's, that he has been guilty himself of what he charges against his daughters. To have a husband and yet to say she loves only her father is no doubt to say "ay" and "no" both at once. But to demand such flattery of your daughters is to be the author rather than the echo of "no good divinity." It is to wish yourself everything and to leave yourself unready for the thunder to refuse your bidding. Lear may not be aware of all he reveals in this speech; but he has discovered that for all his claims to omnipotence, his mortality is as frail as ours.

The second element in Lear's mad discourse, closely related to his running assertion of royal authority, is a pervasive awareness of the worldwide abuse of authority cloaked by deceptive appearances: "see how yond justice rails upon yond simple thief. Hark, in thine ear: change places, and, handy-dandy, which is the justice, which is the thief?" "There thou might'st behold/ The great image of Authority:/ A dog's obey'd in office." "Plate sin with gold,/ And the strong lance of justice hurtless breaks:/ Arm it in rags, a pigmy's straw does pierce it." Third, there is the continuing fixated rage against the wicked daughters: "Down from the waist they are Centaurs,/ Tho women all above." "And when I have stol'n upon these son-in-laws,/ Then kill, kill, kill, kill, kill, kill." Other important ideas emerge at isolated moments in this final madness, but I do not think they affect the crucial interrelationship of the three I have mentioned. Lear keeps shuttling back and forth from his blind assertion of royal potency, to his blinding vision of the corruption of justice by the arbitrary and deceitful use of power, to his limitless rage against the corruption bred of his own loins. None of these elements can be isolated as a "theme" more important than the others; the "theme" of Lear's madness is just the configuration made by all three.[6] Lear sees that of all the rascal beadles, whores, usurers, and cozeners whose corruptions he enumerates, none does offend because he has authorized them. By his first momentary subversion of the traditional doctrine of order, cloaked as it was in the robes of royalty, the king has coined the handy-dandy world in which "ay" and "no" cohabit and justice and thievery are indistinguishable. He keeps insisting that the king cannot be touched for coining; but he keeps seeing horribly what it is he has created, keeps facing the fact attested all round that it *was* his flesh begot those pelican daughters; yet even so, he keeps cursing his daughters through their husbands with "kill, kill, kill." In this total vision Lear is accepting full responsibility for his deed in the most terrifying and purifying fashion that is humanly possible: he responds to its consequences individually full in the face; he confronts and assimilates his tragic error, the world-shaking infection it produced, and his resulting inexpungable hatred of his own flesh.

Two elements are conspicuously missing from Lear's mad discourse. One is self-pity: he no longer talks about his head so old and white, as when buffeted in the storm. The other is a change of heart, an admission that he has taken too little heed of this or that. For Lear now, both self-pity and that deep pity for others expressed by his prayer in the storm are evasions of the crushing responsibility for direct encounter that I have described. Now all Lear does is simply and grandly to face and possess his guilt with a precise enumeration of its consequences and its immutability. He redeems his crime by acknowledging it in the bright uncanny light of his madness, with the human grandeur of Greek tragedy but without the extenuating transparency of Greek reason. In possessing his crime, as in his previous suffering for it, Lear remains that bare, forked animal which is unaccommodated man. And his ability to meet this terrible occasion, to achieve without accommodation of reason the moral coherence and therefore the tragic grandeur of accepting his guilt, reassures us that finally in this world man can be accommodated.

When Lear awakens in Cordelia's tent restored from madness, he is surely not a changed man in the ordinary sense of having a new attitude toward life. From a doctrinal point of view, he has learned nothing, and he subjects Cordelia to a backward version of the play's opening scene:

> *Lear.* Be your tears wet? Yes, faith. I pray weep not.
> If you have poison for me, I will drink it.
> I know you do not love me; for your sisters
> Have, as I do remember, done me wrong.
> You have some cause, they have not.
>
> *Cor.*   No cause, no cause.
>
> (IV.vii.71–75)

Lear is still thinking in those bargain terms by which nature is garnished with invention. First he would trade a kingdom for a pretty speech, then a father's curse for no speech; and now that the wheel of fortune has turned, he is ready to accept poison in payment for his curse. But Cordelia is Cordelia no matter how Fortune turns, and her "no cause" now is the precise equivalent to her "nothing" before. She still loves her father according to her bond, and her next words are, "Will 't please your Highness walk?" Lear is not transfigured by rising to the height of Cordelia's vision of life. He has been barred from that forever by the original mistake ingrained in his character; he can no more learn the lesson of Cordelia than Hamlet learned the lesson of Horatio. Lear is transfigured by kneeling to Cordelia and calling himself "a foolish fond old man." Like Hamlet admiring Horatio, he sees the rightness of her vision of life; then he goes on to accept it on his knees. There he achieves the contrition that has been forged in the heat of his madness.

IV

Lear in his pilgrimage has found no cause in nature for hard hearts or soft. He has found no pattern of patience, no justice, no design, nothing. He has found only himself still insisting upon that royal power through which now he sees how he set the world awry, and still with his sick desire to kill his daughters. Yet in Lear's discovery of himself the play begins to unfold an order in nature wholly independent of the specific requirements of Elizabethan political doctrine. Lear's kneeling to Cordelia after his mind and the world have been tested by chaos begins the return of life to itself. If Lear can never forget that his flesh begot Goneril, at least he now remembers that it made Cordelia too. Beyond the scope of Lear's personal suffering and transfiguration, there are the forces of destruction that his original mistake set loose; and these evil forces in the world, like those within Lear, eventually play themselves out. In *King Lear* evil is self-destructive. Lear's original mistake empowered Edmund and the wicked sisters, and Shakespeare, in building his plot from there, went out of his way in order to assure these evil persons an absolute sway over events, by depriving the good people of the play—Kent, Edgar, and Cordelia—of any power to oppose them or even to console their suffering victims. Yet in the flush of their omnipotence the evil characters turn upon each other and themselves and bring their own wheel of fortune quickly down. The sisters kill each other. Edmund, once divested of his faith in Fortune, is able to recognize his career of evil, and before he dies attempts to rescind his death sentence upon Lear and Cordelia. This general conquest of evil by its own nature, like Lear's victory over himself when he drops to his knees before Cordelia, reassures us with growing conviction that Nature is not capricious, as Edmund had hoped when he identified it with Fortune, nor demonic, as Lear had feared when he ordered Regan to be anatomized, but that Nature is ultimately and just barely providential, restoring order by a process and balance at a cost almost too savage for our vision to endure.

At the heart of this conviction stands Cordelia, whose unshakable adherence to a particular doctrine of order is the play's deepest promise for the renewal of general order. Cordelia no less than Edmund knows the power of Fortune to work capriciously in the world, but that is just why she refuses to depend for life upon whirling stars or turning wheels. She and Kent and Edgar have always known that man can only stand fast for love and justice, enduring a capricious Fortune that may decree at any time his going hence even as his coming hither, if the whole structure of creation is to be maintained. Cordelia's last words in the play, when she has been taken prisoner and is beyond all hope and expectation, might have been spoken with equal relevance when her father disowned her at the beginning:

> We are not the first
> Who with best meaning have incurr'd the worst.
> For thee, oppressed king, am I cast down;
> Myself could else outfrown false Fortune's frown.
> Shall we not see these daughters and these sisters?
> (V.iii.3–7)

From the beginning her meaning has been the best; and her readiness to incur the worst on its behalf succeeds at last, by a hairbreadth, in *rendering* Fortune false by outfrowning its frown. There is something almost savage in Cordelia's speech, which reminds us—like her bristling "Nothing" in the opening scene—just whose daughter she is. We have seen the transfiguring power of her love in the tears and the "No cause, no cause" of her reunion with her father. But now her determination to confront the sisters to whose power she must still submit reminds us by its fury of Lear's curse upon Goneril and of Regan's claws upon Gloucester's eyes. Every member of this family pursues his particular design upon life with remorseless ferocity, Lear unto madness, his daughters unto death. But Cordelia's meaning is the best meaning; if she can pursue it to the same ultimate distance to which Regan does, then it may prevail in the world. In the last line of her speech that is what Cordelia does: she announces herself ready for that death which, when it comes, will be as gratuitous as Regan's, and will thereby constitute the necessary living proof that men must endure even their going hence so that man in his goodness may prevail. Cordelia's death, in all its motiveless benignity, is essential to Shakespeare's purpose: it completes what Lear's kneeling began and what Edmund's conversion enlarged, the revelation by *King Lear* of a need for order in the human community, and an enabling goodness at the heart of Nature that cannot be overthrown.

Yet that supreme revelation, for all the thoroughness with which we have seen it achieved, brings with it very little sense of human triumph. We like to say that tragedy affirms the moral order of the universe and thereby reconciles us to life. In the process it normally exalts us with a feeling of wonder, to balance that great woe which, like blind Gloucester confronting mad Lear, we have seen feelingly. When Hamlet and Othello ask at the end to have their stories told, it is not for the sake of preserving among mankind their brightly polished memories. It is rather to convey the wonder of that divinity which has shaped this end, in spite of, and yet by means of, the vagaries of fortune. Through the wonder of the hero's story we may apprehend the grandeur of human life even while facing the scene of death;[7] and this total vision uplifts our spirit. But at the end of *King Lear* there is no request for the hero's story. The characters stand dumbly surrounding the dead father and daughter, asking whether this is the end of the world that was always foretold. They do not include even a possible audience for the hero's story among the lords and ladies of the country. They are only those who have lived the story themselves—Kent, who now wants to die, and Edgar, who will be brief and then silent. For us there is no hint of wonder to be had in this scene, and barely an ounce of reconciliation with life. "Vex not his

ghost," and "He but usurp'd his life," are the last words spoken
about Lear, and they have nothing in them of sweet princes
sung to rest by angels. Edgar, whose function in this scene
parallels Horatio's at the end of *Hamlet,* does not, like Horatio,
spend twenty lines in preparing the others to hear the hero's
story; he closes the play by telling quickly why no story can
be told:

> The weight of this sad time we must obey,
> Speak what we feel, not what we ought to say.
> The oldest have borne most; we that are young
> Shall never see so much, nor live so long.
> (V.iii.323–26)

What we really feel is that the young are prematurely aged,
that life itself has grown old. We and Edgar have borne witness
in this theater for as long as it has taken for the oldest to bear
the most; and we are all as much depleted as the oldest. In
King Lear life has been tested to its limit; it has had to spend
itself wholly in order to affirm itself at all, and the result, no
wonder, is exhaustion.

We become depressed when we are emotionally spent, and I
think the depression that so often follows *King Lear* is responsible for some common pessimistic misreadings of the play. Each
of the following quotations from *King Lear* has sometime been
proposed as a summation of the play:

> As flies to wanton boys are we to th' gods.
> They kill us for their sport.   (IV.i.36–37)

> Humanity must perforce prey on itself,
> Like monsters of the deep.   (IV.ii.49–50)

> O ruin'd piece of nature! This great world
> Shall so wear out to nought.   (IV.vi.137–38)

But each of these possibilities has been suggested only to make
its rejection the more clear and convincing. The play does finally
discover a profound impetus for order in the universe and,
because of that, the possibility of man's deliverance from evil
through the rectitude and love that are capable of renewing

that order. Furthermore, the discovery is made through Shakespeare's final affirmation of his own local doctrine of order: *King Lear* affirms universal order in the particular terms of its own culture, just as Sophoclean tragedy had done. I said earlier that the history plays and *Hamlet* converge upon *King Lear* from different directions, presenting it with the problem of order on the one hand and the problem of conduct on the other. *King Lear* resolves both problems in a form that is final for Shakespeare, by linking them together and showing that order is necessary to life and is made possible by those who suffer Fortune through. We are inevitably tempted to suppose that a play that joins and then resolves the two problems with which Shakespeare had been most deeply concerned in his earlier work marks the culmination of his whole intellectual development.

Yet any such inference runs hard into that heavy final scene. Cordelia's death guarantees the order of nature and the state by the final answer it gives to Hamlet's question of whether to be or not to be. But of Cordelia's death Kent asks, "Is this the promis'd end?"; and we must ask that question of Shakespeare concerning the play of *King Lear*. To see the play reject its potentially most extreme pessimism, and to feel in that rejection the power with which order and patience are affirmed, is not necessarily to accept order and patience as the most constructive values in human life. We may hope for more, because order and patience are often means to more wondrous ends, and because Shakespeare in fact went on to write plays that end more in wonder than does *King Lear*. The exhaustion we feel at the end of *King Lear* is related to the fact that although evil has proved self-destructive, it has brought down good with it; though Cordelia's ability to outface Fortune has held open the possibility of order in the world, in the process she has used her life to sustain order instead of letting order nourish life. It may be that men must endure their going hence even as their coming hither; but that fortitude, we must continue to hope, should be incidental to more vivid and varied pursuits, and not itself become the center and aim of our existence. It is not that Cordelia and Kent and Edgar are merely passive in their suffering and therefore boring. What leaves us finally mute and shaken is that all their strenuous activity has been devoted to the minimal end of keeping life together at all. The whole play is a great affirmation, but it affirms only that life is not nothing, that life is livable and may go on. As John Holloway has written,

> . . . if the play advances a "positive," I think it is that when men turn away from how they should live, there are forces in life which constrain them to return. In this play love is not a "victory"; it is not that which stands at "the centre of the action," and without which "life is meaningless"; it does not rule creation. If anything rules creation, it is (though only, as it were, by a hairsbreadth) simply rule itself. What order restores, is order. Men tangle their lives; life, at a price, is self-untangling at last.[8]

It is fitting that Shakespeare's greatest play should make that discovery with overwhelming clarity. But it is natural to ask, once we are assured that life can be lived, how we can live it in its full richness; and I believe Shakespeare goes on to ask that question in *Antony and Cleopatra* and the last plays.

We can see how *King Lear* leaves this question open by looking at two of Lear's speeches toward the end of the play. At the climax of his madness, just before Cordelia's servants find him, Lear makes a speech that is unprecedented for him, both in its awareness of his surroundings and in its thought:

> If thou wilt weep my fortunes, take my eyes.
> I know thee well enough; thy name is Gloucester.
> Thou must be patient. We came crying hither;
> Thou know'st, the first time that we smell the air
> We wawl and cry. I will preach to thee. Mark.
> .   .   .   .
> When we are born, we cry that we are come
> To this great stage of fools. This' a good block.
> It were a delicate stratagem to shoe
> A troop of horse with felt. I'll put 't in proof,
> And when I have stol'n upon these sons-in-law,
> Then, kill, kill, kill, kill, kill, kill!
>
> (IV.vi.180–91)

The first part of this speech echoes Hamlet's "readiness is all" and Edgar's "Ripeness is all" speeches; it names the ethic by which Cordelia has lived and will soon die. But the second part of the speech contradicts the first and proposes a Machiavellian stratagem by which to take revenge upon the wicked daughters, so that both parts together reopen the question of Hamlet's soliloquy: whether to suffer outrageous fortune or to take arms against one's troubles. During the time of his dependency upon Goneril and Regan, Lear vacillated between these alternatives in action, just as Hamlet did in thought; and now, though his madness is almost spent and his tragic self-knowledge secured, still he cannot settle upon one or the other. Soon he is reunited with Cordelia, for whom the issue has never been in question; and when they have been captured and Cordelia affirms her ethic by asking fiercely, "Shall we not see these daughters and these sisters?", Lear replies quickly:

> No, no, no, no! Come, let's away to prison.
> We two alone will sing like birds i' th' cage.
> When thou dost ask me blessing, I'll kneel down
> And ask of thee forgiveness. So we'll live,
> And pray, and sing, and tell old tales, and laugh
> At gilded butterflies, and hear poor rogues
> Talk of court news; and we'll talk with them too—
> Who loses and who wins; who's in, who's out—
> And take upon 's the mystery of things,
> As if we were God's spies; and we'll wear out,
> In a wall'd prison, packs and sects of great ones
> That ebb and flow by th' moon.   (V.iii.8–19)

This speech, so beautiful and redeeming in its own terms, also marks a crucial moment in Shakespeare's development. Lear's final wish is neither to suffer Fortune's blows nor to take up arms against her, but to transcend a world in which that is the choice. On the one hand, the speech looks back both to Lear's raving about the deceptiveness of appearance and the corruption of justice, and to Hamlet's contempt of the world. In a sense Lear ends where Hamlet began when he lamented the unprofitable uses of this world. Yet Lear's tone, which begins to sound like the last plays, has in it none of Hamlet's disgust; and the idea leads him not to a yearning for death but to a continuing desire to bear witness to the character of human life, so long as he can be protected by prison against its dangers.

In short, Lear's willingness to accept now the fallen uses of this world against which he railed in his madness, and therefore to desire transcendence in life rather than death, looks straight forward to *Antony and Cleopatra*. Life must go on, the restored Lear knows, even in a world bound to fall again and again into disorder and corruption; life *can* go on in such a world, the play has taught us, because of the goodness in need of order that is also bound up in the heart of things. Despite all he has seen and suffered, Lear is still anxious to talk to poor rogues full of court news; yet he needs the protection of his walled prison, for all that he is turned back toward life, and we cannot blame him for that. Thus, the question with which he leaves us is whether this privileged view can be made good in the world; whether it is not noblest of all to endure the vicissitudes of Fortune as a means and not an end; whether man may not actively mitigate the evil in the world by infusing it with good from moment to moment rather than by enduring its ravages until both are spent; whether man, having secured his being out of nothingness, may not go on to make for himself a burgeoning place in creation. And these are questions for *Antony and Cleopatra*.

In *King Lear* the problem of order is not solved in the usual sense, for no way has been discovered to ignore disorder as a continuing potentiality of human life. But the play has shown how order is continually restored no matter what the human cost, for order is the necessary basis for life and from now on, for Shakespeare, may be assumed as given. *Antony and Cleopatra* goes on to inquire what life may be lived on that basis; and one further aspect of the connection between the two plays must be mentioned here. In an earlier chapter I spoke of the method of discontinuity in *Antony and Cleopatra,* a procedure by which the causal relationships among actions and events are suppressed, and hence, in effect, denied. That procedure may be observed occasionally in Shakespeare's earlier plays, but I think its first significant and organic use is to be found in *King Lear*. The crucial events of both the beginning and the end of *King Lear* are wholly gratuitous from the standpoint either of general probability or of the specific dramatic context. Lear's decision to divide the kingdom according to his daughters' speeches comes as a surprise to everybody; and the fact that Cordelia and Kent, who are most unsettled by it, were previously Lear's favorites shows how capriciously "out of character" his decision is. At the end of the play Edmund's delay in rescinding the death sentence after his change of heart is just as maddeningly unmotivated. Between this beginning and end there are many gratuitous actions: for example, Edgar's acquiescence in his father's judgment against him without confronting his father directly; Gloucester's wish to go all the way to Dover simply in order to commit suicide; Edgar's refusal to identify himself to his father on the way to Dover; Kent's similar refusal to make himself known to Lear; and the confrontation between blind Gloucester and mad Lear.[9] These are not mere discrepancies in the structure of the plot, although there are many of those too; they are not subordinate pieces that Shakespeare failed inadvertently to fit together tightly. All of these actions go to show the creative power of the good to suffer meaningfully; they are the means by which the plot tells us through its very structure that man must be ready to endure the utmost. Hence these actions are among the principal structures of which the whole framework of the play is wrought; and yet they are free-standing, disconnected from each other and from all causes. We cannot regard them as defects in Shakespeare's technique for which we need to apologize disingenuously by claiming that *King Lear* is too big for the stage. Shakespeare has begun to evolve here a new technique of discontinuity, which, there is good reason to suppose, reflects a new dimension in his vision of the world.

That new dimension originates, I suggest, in Cordelia's words, "No cause, no cause." Cordelia lives and dies on behalf of a world in which justice and love are not bargained for but freely given. In order for such a world to exist, *King Lear* has painfully discovered, evil must be given its due and allowed its unmotived sway. Evil and good, disorder as well as order, are fixed potentialities of human life, and do not exist in causal relations with each other. Each is self-generating, and each act of generation is discontinuous with all others. The failure of Edgar and Kent to reveal themselves to those whom they never fail to serve is the necessary visible means by which good must causelessly reconstitute itself in a world dominated by an equally self-renewing evil. This ability of good to begin again and again in discontinuous moments keeps the world of *King Lear* from being wholly reduced to chaos by the evil forces that control it. It now remains to be seen whether the relationship can be reversed, and good in its endlessly renewed beginnings can dominate a world in which evil yet endures by redeeming evil from moment to moment. If, as I have suggested, *King Lear* bequeaths that problem to *Antony and Cleopatra,* then by the technique of discontinuity, appropriate to a world beyond good and evil and hence beyond cause, *King Lear* has made ready for *Antony and Cleopatra* the principal means by which to undertake its task.

CHAPTER FIVE

THE IDEAL OF ORDER SURPASSED:
RESOLUTION AND APOTHEOSIS IN
ANTONY AND CLEOPATRA

ROM THE TIME of Antony's return from Egypt until the end of the play, Shakespeare elaborates the vision he had achieved in *King Lear* in the climactic action of *Antony and Cleopatra*. There are no villains here, no separate forces of evil in the world. Octavius and Cleopatra are not Antony's enemies in any usual sense but only, in their different ways, his occasions for becoming an enemy to himself. Good and evil are seen as related aspects of his undivided being, and their conflict with each other is endlessly renewed from moment to moment. The technique of discontinuity shapes the whole play, with its enormous number of separate "scenes," brought together only as a series and not as a linked chain of cause and effect. Now upon the slightest leverage Antony swings between the most distant polarities of conduct and attitude, from his honorable dare to Caesar to settle their differences in single combat to his shameful retreat at Actium in pursuit of the fleeing Cleopatra. And for every mistake he makes, we are told repeatedly by Antony as well as others, there is only one reason: Antony has violated his own identity. From moment to moment he gains and loses and regains himself, always wrestling with his own nature, full of unalterable propensities for folly as well as heroism.

Lear, for all his final contrition, cannot change himself; but after what he has suffered, he needs his walled prison to protect him from further incitements of his own nature as well as from the world. Antony takes the next step, and without such protection risks his equally human frailty amidst the uses of the world, where he tries to make good his mistakes from moment to moment by becoming continuously responsible for his own nature. In this process Antony goes beyond contrition to magnanimity. He keeps giving of his treasure and his spirit, not in a grandiose gesture at the end but in repetitive discrete actions, to those who have no claim on him as well as to those whom his folly has hurt. Antony is spiritually elevated to a vision that is incomprehensible to the other characters, even while it continues to inspire, or to restore, their enormous loyalty to him. In the last half of the play we see Shakespeare moving toward that comprehension of life which is characteristic of his last plays; and we might say of the later Antony, changing only the sexual designation, what Florizel says to Perdita in *The Winter's Tale*:

> Each your doing,
> So singular in each particular,
> Crowns what you are doing in the present deed
> That all your acts are queens.   (IV.iv.143–46)

To follow Antony here (and Cleopatra later), is to follow the moral process by which one outgrows the politics of order. After his return to Egypt and for the rest of his life, Antony is unable to pursue an outwardly consistent or a politically responsible line of conduct. Although the reason of mankind sits in the wind against him, at Actium he decides to fight Octavius at sea rather than on land where his forces are more experienced. When in the midst of that battle he is about to defy all prophecy and win, he turns and retreats to follow the frightened Cleopatra. Immediately he falls into violent recriminations over his cowardly act, first with himself and then with Cleopatra. But upon a hint from her, he refurbishes his limitless confidence and calls for wine once again. His poise is no sooner regained than it is freshly blasted by what he takes to be Cleopatra's flirtation with Thyreus. After he has Thyreus whipped and scolds Cleopatra, she charms him anew; and he orders a feast to celebrate their newly reassured love. The feast is followed by a great victory over Caesar by land, and this is followed by another ignoble defeat at sea, where once again Cleopatra betrays him. Finally, when he is full of rage at his "Triple-turn'd whore," she sends the false report of her death and he kills himself.

As if the significance of these events for Antony's moral degeneration were not self-evident, his life is played out to the accompaniment of an eloquent chorus, whose chief voice is Enobarbus, explaining in minute detail the irrational effeminacy of Antony's every act. Maecenas and Caesar, the anonymous soldier who warns against fighting by sea, the once-loyal deserter Canidius, and the ever-loyal Scarus and Eros, all testify, step by step, to Antony's mounting folly. Enobarbus speaks for them all in those speeches by which he persuades himself to leave Antony:

> Yes, like enough high-battled Caesar will
> Unstate his happiness and be stag'd to th' show
> Against a sworder! I see men's judgments are
> A parcel of their fortunes, and things outward
> Do draw the inward quality after them
> To suffer all alike. That he should dream,
> Knowing all measures, the full Caesar will
> Answer his emptiness! Caesar, thou hast subdu'd
> His judgment too. (III.xiii.29–37)

> Now he'll outstare the lightning. To be furious
> Is to be frighted out of fear, and in that mood
> The dove will peck the estridge. I see still
> A diminution in our captain's brain
> Restores his heart. When valour preys on reason,
> It eats the sword it fights with. I will seek
> Some way to leave him. (III.xiii.195–201)

Yet there is something strained in the tone of this chorus, although it appears to speak the inescapable dictates of reason. Its voice is too pat, all too predictably eloquent; its opinions are so transparent, so neatly justified, that we cannot help feeling that Antony's critics protest too much. And we finally discover the meaning and relevance of all their choric commentary not in Antony's death but in that of Enobarbus. Enobarbus has remained loyal to Antony longer than any of the principal spokesmen for reason and sound policy, and yet he discovers finally that his loyalty has been too short-lived. He voices at the end a choric commentary upon the chorus, which devaluates entirely the kind of reason for which that chorus has consistently spoken.

It has been observed that the Fool in *King Lear* passes out of the play at the point where Lear enters a realm of experience that the Fool's mind and heart are not large enough to master. This also happens to Enobarbus. He has been all along the penetrating voice of reason, the hard-bitten realist who strips away the façade of hypocrisy, self-deception, and false appearance from the public world. But the reason on whose behalf he has spoken turns out to be mere timeserving policy designed to preserve the order of the state as this play conceives it by maintaining the existing balance of power between Antony and Octavius. Enobarbus now discovers that this reason must finally prey on itself, that Octavius, for all the worldly success of his shrewd policy, is a more erratic, irresponsible, and dishonorable master than Antony:

> Alexas did revolt and went to Jewry on
> Affairs of Antony; there did dissuade
> Great Herod to incline himself to Caesar
> And leave his master Antony. For this pains
> Caesar hath hang'd him. Canidius and the rest
> That fell away have entertainment, but
> No honourable trust. I have done ill,
> Of which I do accuse myself so sorely
> That I will joy no more.   (IV.vi.12–20)

Octavius is no villain but, like King Henry V, whom he so resembles in character, the agent of political order renewing itself. Sir Thomas North said it was "predestinated" that all the world should fall into his hands and a long period of calm and order be restored to Rome. But the morality of Octavius' world now resembles that of the villains in *King Lear,* under whose dominance humanity must prey upon itself. Enobarbus finally understands that the reason that had been his "safer guide" is no longer relevant to his experience; and without a deeper vision of the world, he is lost. Enobarbus is re-enacting the experience of Octavia, who also had to fade out of the play, because her scope of vision permitted her only to flutter helplessly between her brother and her husband, like a straw in the wind.

But where Octavia left the play in ignorance, it is given to Enobarbus to discover before he dies the limits of his vision. In the speech I have quoted, he decides to make the best of his bad bargain and spend his remaining days in timeserving, even if it will bring him no joy. Then Antony sends back his treasure, apparently once again letting "valour" prey upon "reason"; this time Enobarbus understands that he has not simply made an error in judgment but that his very grounds of judgment have become dwarfed and irrelevant. He understands that there is something ultimate to choose between Antony and Octavius. If from the limited standpoint of that reason which he has served Antony has performed a gratuitous act, that act serves nevertheless a deeper rationality than he has known. Antony's magnanimity reflects an unspoiled rectitude of private feeling insisting upon expression in public life, despite all embarrassments. No society, either in history or fiction, has been able to afford the luxury of generosity toward traitors; no private man who is ready to kiss away kingdoms and provinces may be expected to bother one way or another about the treasure of a single citizen. In sending back Enobarbus' treasure, Antony had said, "Say that I wish he never find more cause/ To change a master," with precise respect for Enobarbus' desertion and with humble readiness to acknowledge his own lapse. But the very form of Antony's acknowledgment, the return of the treasure, transforms his lapse into transcendent virtue. Enobarbus recognizes that Antony is not simply taking public occasion to indulge his sentimentality but that he is now observing a public honor inseparable from his personal morality. With this new measure of his own dishonor, Enobarbus will die of a broken heart; but first he rises to the occasion given him by Antony: he coins his own epitaph out of two words that he wrenches into an equivalence of meaning that reflects in turn the synonymy of public and private judgments. He calls himself finally a "master-leaver and a fugitive."

The chorus thereby ends on a different note than that on which it began. It has come to perceive that Antony has entered a human condition invulnerable to judgment by the timeserving world of political order. We must now look directly at Antony's later career, beginning with his choice to fight at Actium by sea. It is a common assumption that Antony is misled by Cleopatra into making this decision. But Shakespeare takes considerable pains to exclude this possibility and to show that Antony makes up his mind without consulting Cleopatra.

Ant. Is it not strange, Canidius,
That from Tarentum and Brundusium
He could so quickly cut the Ionian sea
And take in Toryne?—You have heard on't, sweet?

Cleo. Celerity is never more admir'd
Than by the negligent.

Ant. A good rebuke,
Which might have well becom'd the best of men
To taunt at slackness. Canidius, we
Will fight with him by sea.

Cleo. By sea? What else?

Can. Why will my lord do so?

Ant. For that he dares us to't.

Eno. So hath my lord dar'd him to single fight.

Can. Ay, and to wage this battle at Pharsalia,
Where Caesar fought with Pompey. But these offers,
Which serve not for his vantage, he shakes off;
And so should you.   (III.vii.21–35)

This passage marks the beginning of the end, and it captures in microcosm the essential quality and meaning of Antony's final realm of life. Cleopatra urges him to action, but she has been so little consulted that she is surprised to discover that Antony, unlike herself, did not take for granted a battle at sea. Far from influencing his decision, she is surprised that he still needs to make a decision. The choice between land and sea simply is not real to her, and the fact that it remains a pressing choice for Antony indicates how little he is influenced by her judgment or caprice. It is part of Antony's manliness that he can accept with a whole and humble heart Cleopatra's criticism of his "slackness," and then turn in full authority to consult with Canidius about a problem of strategy that he does not regard as properly her concern.

There is no reason, then, to doubt the accuracy of Antony's own explanation of his decision to fight by sea: "For that he dares us to't." If he was eager to challenge Octavius to single combat in the knowledge that he is the better swordsman, it is only appropriate that he accept Octavius' dare and risk a fight at sea where he has reason to think his opponent the better naval tactician. Antony not only accepts in Egypt his continuing obligation of Roman honor, he enhances that honor by investing it with a final meaning. Shakespeare now develops his most elaborate contrast between the timeserving policy of Octavius, which is "predestinated" to preserve the order of the state because it is aimed carefully at his "vantage," and the timeless honor of Antony, which outstrips the requirements of any possible doctrine of order in the state. Antony, so to speak, platonizes the conflict between himself and Octavius. He projects intact their present balance of power upon a transcendental battleground of moral values: he will endure voluntarily the unpredictable blows of fortune, in the form of Octavius' navy, even if Octavius will not risk his sword. Though it makes no practical difference where their duel is held, Antony proposes to fight Octavius "at Pharsalia/ Where Caesar fought with Pompey," as if to achieve a symbolic revenge for the young Caesar's betrayal of the young Pompey. In his earlier peace negotiations with Pompey, Antony did not underestimate his opponent's prowess by sea but declared himself nevertheless ready to risk a sea battle. Then he went on to remind Pompey of the triumvirs' strength by land and to conclude a peace negotiated on the basis of each party's recognition of the other's position of superior strength. His effort to make war with

Octavius on the same basis constitutes the most scrupulous possible defense of that Roman honor which he earned in the negotiations with Pompey, and which Octavius betrayed by ruining Pompey in his grinding pursuit of power.

In *King Lear,* I argued, the ability of the good characters to endure the ravages of fortune even unto death, although it answers Hamlet's question of what it means to really live, still does not comprise for Shakespeare the ultimate power or the human value of life. Now we begin to see why. Although the good characters of *King Lear* are active, not passive, their activity only goes to prove that life has meaning and is therefore possible. Antony's willingness to risk a sea battle is not merely for the sake of defending the order of the world, his own place in it, and thereby the minimal meaning of life. That kind of action is now seen as only the protection of fortuitous, and hence irrelevant, worldly advantages. Antony's action is more disinterested than that; it is action undertaken for the wholly gratuitous reason that Octavius dares him to it. This voluntary submission to the uncertainties of fortune transforms endurance into magnanimity and infuses all of life with the particular meaning of Antony's new honor. Antony's submission generates new possibilities for life, and then goes on to value these possibilities according to the most rigorous ethical standards. Where Cordelia's necessary endurance was conservative, Antony's voluntary submission is creative. It brings new dimensions of right conduct into the range of possibility and thereby offers man new chances to make his own world. Cleopatra said at the beginning that she would "set a bourn how far to be belov'd"; and Antony told her she would then have to find new heaven and new earth. Now, in his insistence on the inmost meaning of Roman honor as the basis for his Egyptian strategy, Antony is beginning the search himself.

He is not only submitting himself to the most disinterested standard of Roman virtue but, at the same time, is reversing the process and painfully incorporating his union with Cleopatra in his affirmation of public values. From the beginning, of course, these public and private considerations have been connected for him: his liaison with Cleopatra has been the proximate cause of the civil war. But during this last residence in Egypt, just as in Rome before, he tries to outstrip the time-serving world of proximate causes. A man of worldly discretion, concerned immediately with his "vantage," would have listened to the choric exponents of reason who warned against Cleopatra's participation in the war. He would have ordered her to her boudoir to await the outcome in the company of a eunuch. But for Antony now, war must be the immediate and complete expression of his love as well as his honor. Just as he needs to risk Octavius' navy, so he is ready to have Cleopatra at his side in the sea battle; and later he will have her perform Eros' function of buckling on his armor for the land battle. Cleopatra is becoming a symbol for Antony in the same way that Pharsalia is a symbol: he can avenge Pompey with nothing less than a full public assertion of his love, and the assertion of love will make the revenge providential. Antony is approaching that heady vision in which his public and private lives are necessary conditions for each other.

On the two occasions when Antony now loses his head, in his shameful retreat at Actium and his shameless whipping of Thyreus, he thinks Cleopatra has betrayed him, and immediately he defaults. He rejects the obligation to finish a battle once begun and the simple duty of courtesy toward a messenger. But in neither case does he lose his head simply in order to follow the dissolute promptings of his heart; it is rather as if Cleopatra's defection has made his whole enterprise for the moment irrelevant. His public aspirations, because he has purified them of mundane desires, are meaningless when they do not include his affections; and if he cannot have both, he will not have either.

When Antony scolds Cleopatra for leading him after her retreating form at Actium, she apologizes and says she did not think he would have followed. But she must have hoped so. Her insistence first on participating and then on running from the battle scene is of a piece with all her efforts to beguile Antony by momentary reversals of mood and behavior. She is always trying to keep him "uncaught" by "the world's great snare." That is after all what it means to be Cleopatra. Similarly, when Antony scolds her for flirting with Thyreus, she says, "Not know me yet?", and launches into the great speech that shows her passion for Antony to be deeper than ever, precisely because she has manipulated Thyreus. Cleopatra betrays him, no doubt, according to the single standard of Rome, but only by insisting upon that other standard which has made Egypt a pre-eminent value for him. Antony recognizes this fact in both episodes, accepts Cleopatra's explanations, and affirms for himself her Egyptian meaning by calling each time for wine and kisses.

But he does not go on to think himself released from the Roman standard to which he has now aspired, and he keeps taxing himself for his own action, "Stroy'd in dishonour." Antony must have both worlds now, Rome and Egypt. Octavius, in refusing the duel, and Cleopatra, in running from the naval battle, both obstruct him, each one pursuing only the "vantage" of his single meaning and thereby challenging Antony constantly to choose either one or the other. But Antony keeps moving back and forth, even here in Egypt, trying to encompass both; and this oscillating action becomes the locus of his final suffering and glory. One source of his suffering is that Octavius and Cleopatra leave him no room even to articulate his deepening vision. Another is his inability to make good that vision in continuous action, and hence his moment-to-moment maiming of one part or the other of his emergent identity. Nevertheless, his glory arises from that courage to be himself and spend himself which results from this failure, and which produces finally, if impermanently, the dazzling success of the land battle, with its confirming unification of Antony's manifold aspirations.

No major Shakespearean hero is so eloquent and severe in judging himself as the later Antony. Beside Antony's self-recriminations, the lesson of Lear's madness seems partial, and even Macbeth's celebrated conscience looks incomplete. Antony reproves himself with a thoroughness and clarity that make the later choric comments of Enobarbus and the others merely redundant:

Ant.	Hark! the land bids me tread no more upon't!
	It is asham'd to bear me! Friends, come hither.
	I am so lated in the world that I
	Have lost my way for ever. I have a ship
	Laden with gold. Take that; divide it. Fly,
	And make your peace with Caesar.
All.	Fly? not we!
Ant.	I have fled myself, and have instructed cowards
	To run and show their shoulders. Friends, be gone.—
	I have myself resolv'd upon a course
	Which has no need of you. (III.xi.1–10)

He goes on to rail against Octavius and Cleopatra, to be sure; but he comes back again and again to himself, subjecting his own conduct to the same criteria that prompted his offer to fight Octavius and his challenge to single combat. He never justifies his lapse at sea on the grounds that Octavius has refused the duel; and he never claims that the world is well lost for love, nor for the sake of that transcendental realm of experience which he does not know he has entered. Instead, he blames himself for "rashness" on the one hand and for "fear and doting" on the other, thus anticipating precisely Enobarbus' later charge that his valor preys upon reason. He admits that his sword has been "made weak by my affection." But he does not stop even with these concessions to the worldly wisdom of all who have warned and criticized him. He goes on to invest his self-reproval with the same final meaning that characterized his original aspirations. He repeats to his followers, "Let that be left/ Which leaves itself," (III.xi.19–20) and to himself, "I have offended reputation—/ A most unnoble swerving." (III.xi.49–50) In these remarks he is putting to its absolute test that whole vision by which he has taken the measure of Octavius' and Cleopatra's single halves: he is using it to measure himself.

Antony's ability to subject himself to this kind of judgment shows another facet of Shakespeare's advance beyond *King Lear*. During the course of his life Lear undergoes a linear process of education, during which he learns through his madness the nature and consequences of his offense, and then acknowledges his lesson by kneeling to Cordelia. The process had a clearly marked beginning, and it has a visible ending, after which Lear is ready to give up the world for love, and live out his days with Cordelia in the transcendence of his walled prison. But when Antony says at Actium, "I have offended reputation—/ A most unnoble swerving," his education is finished, even though the play, and his life in the play, are still *in medias res*. He had achieved something comparable to Lear's knowledge by the time he left Rome to return to Egypt, where he has no pride to be chastened nor conduct to unlearn; the moment he gets back to Egypt, he is challenging Octavius to the duel and accepting the dare to a sea fight. He keeps making mistakes, but his mistakes are beyond regretting, and beyond any sort of final remorse that might be symbolized by kneeling or a bird cage, because they are themselves the ongoing consequences of his new aspirations. Antony is free, so to speak, to locate himself simultaneously in the timeserving world and the timeless cosmos, to go beyond Lear and expose himself directly to an ultimate judgment. Having done so, he does not need to reject the world as Lear does, to flatter the gods from a safe port. After his defeat at Actium, to be sure, he does once request of Caesar that he be released from this world and be allowed to live "A private man at Athens." But that is the lapse that proves the rule. Caesar rejects this request, and sends his messenger to "Observe how Antony becomes his flaw." Antony is projected back into the world, where we now see him repeat his challenge to a duel and then order the whipping of Thyreus, thus becoming his virtue and his flaw alternately and endlessly. He is held within the world to keep on daring life and suffering all, not in madness but in the bright daylight knowledge of himself alternately leaving himself and then returning. Antony must go on suffering, but he suffers whole in the self-knowledge and self-reproval that lead to his final magnanimity and transfiguration.

There is also in the process of Antony's passion something that looks like, and yet goes beyond, the self-deception that I have traced in Shakespeare's earlier protagonists. Amid his self-reproval, Antony keeps reminding himself and us of his former glory as "the greatest prince o' th' world." He looks back nostalgically to the old Antony of reputation:

> Look thou say
> He makes me angry with him; for he seems
> Proud and disdainful, harping on what I am,
> Not what he knew I was. He makes me angry;
> And at this time most easy 'tis to do 't,
> When my good stars that were my former guides
> Have empty left their orbs and shot their fires
> Into th' abysm of hell.   (III.xiii.140–47)

But in these consolatory references to his past, and there are many others, Antony does not evade the ethical demands of the present through a false image of himself. He knows that the past is indeed past, and he speaks repeatedly of the decline in his present fortunes. But even in the teeth of adverse fortune he tries to earn in the present the reputation of the past. His good stars may have shot their fires into hell, but in so doing they have left empty their orbs, which need to be refilled; he attempts to meet this need by his renewed challenge to Octavius for single combat and by his insistence upon coming back fighting, once Cleopatra has replenished him after the defeat at Actium. His consolatory speeches are not stages in the creation of a false image of himself that will enable him to ignore his debacle, like Richard II's, for example, or Lear's at the beginning; they are rather the final stages of recognition that began with self-reproval and that lead to that bounteous sharing of himself with others, both in strength and weakness, into which self-dramatization has now been transformed. From Actium onward Antony is unable to hide from himself. He has discovered the meeting ground between his two worlds; and if he is thwarted in his effort to occupy that ground, he is nevertheless unable to return to that stage of circumscribed awareness whose sign is self-deception. He cannot cheer himself up, as the earlier protagonists managed to do, because his unfulfilled aspirations have been so much more inclusive than theirs. He has been willing to risk all the selfhood that they tried to protect by self-dramatization, and this now earns him that creative enlargement of selfhood in magnanimity which becomes his final identity.

That identity is achieved in the whole action surrounding Antony's land victory that precedes his final defeat at sea. This begins with a last meal, where he shakes hands with all his servants and thinks to change places with them, like the dragonish cloud changing its visible shape:

Ant.   And thou art honest too.
          I wish I could be made so many men,
          And all of you clapp'd up together in
          An Antony, that I might do you service
          So good as you have done.

All.   The gods forbid!

Ant.   Well, my good fellows, wait on me to-night.
          Scant not my cups, and make as much of me
          As when my empire was your fellow too
          And suffer'd my command.   (IV.ii.15–23)

Cleopatra, observing this episode, is baffled by Antony's conduct; Enobarbus explains, with his characteristic final irrelevance, that Antony's motive is to make his followers weep. But at this point Antony is no more making a false appeal for sympathy than he is feeling sorry for himself. He is only voicing that same spirit in which, after Actium, he offered a treasure ship and safe-conduct to any soldiers who wished to leave him now that he had left himself. And his servants now, like his soldiers before, will not hear of any scheme to stifle their service or limit their devotion. Kent in *King Lear* has the double office of trying to persuade Lear of his folly and yet to maintain his own perfect fealty no matter how Lear's folly promotes the ruin of all men's fortunes. Kent's unshakable loyalty reflects grandly upon Lear, but yet we give its full credit to Kent himself, whom we admire more lovingly than any other servant Shakespeare created. Antony's servants, on the other hand, have not needed to teach him his folly: he has seen it himself, and he has had the manliness to acknowledge it to them. The credit for his anonymous servants' devotion then goes to Antony: their perfect loyalty is only the reflection of Antony's self-knowledge and humility in all its creative power. As John Middleton Murry has said,

> This is the point at which the superhuman becomes human. The royalty that draws loyalty to it, that compels loyalty indeed, but by an internal, not an external, compulsion, whereby the servant is at once the lover and the friend, and knows that he becomes his own true self only in serving his lord—this royalty is, in the lord himself, superhuman. It cannot be acquired by taking thought: it *is*. It expects allegiance, as the earth expects rain.[1]

This royalty, as an existential fact that we have witnessed Antony bring into being irrespective of any particular doctrine of order, now becomes the single source and the only result of his victory on land. Shakespeare now takes pains, in the arrangement of his materials, to denude this victory of every temporal cause and result. The banquet scene from which I have quoted is followed immediately by that mystical night scene where Antony's soldiers hear the music of hautboys under the stage and realize that "the god Hercules, whom Antony lov'd,/ Now leaves him." The next morning, while preparing for battle, Antony hears of Enobarbus' desertion, which Shake-speare has put off until this moment—although Enobarbus had announced his intention before the previous night's banquet—as if to double the effect of Antony's desertion by his beloved god Hercules. Antony had said after Actium, "I am so lated in the world that I/ Have lost my way for ever." But in this final isolation that precedes the land battle, where he is thrown back only upon himself and Cleopatra, he finds his way at last. Cleopatra replaces Eros as his valet, and readies him in her boudoir, so to speak, for his "royal occupation." She buckles on his armor better than Eros does, and yet he insists that her essential function is only to be the "armourer of my heart." Not recklessly and yet joyously, he goes off to battle, where he hears of Enobarbus' desertion, blames himself, and orders the return of Enobarbus' treasure. Next comes Enobarbus' acknowledgement of *his* mistake, and then, as if in answer to Enobarbus, Antony's victory over Caesar's land army.

Antony announces that victory with a speech in which he regards his soldiers' triumph over the enemy as a result of their inner triumph over themselves, a transcendence of timeserving, in which public and private aspirations have been unified. The army itself has achieved for this moment what Antony aspired to by his challenge to single combat and his submission to a sea fight:

> We have beat him to his camp. Run one before
> And let the queen know of our gests. To-morrow,
> Before the sun shall see's, we'll spill the blood
> That has to-day escap'd. I thank you all;
> For doughty-handed are you, and have fought
> Not as you serv'd the cause, but as't had been
> Each man's like mine. You have shown all Hectors.
> Enter the city, clip your wives, your friends,
> Tell them your feats, whilst they with joyful tears
> Wash the congealment from your wounds and kiss
> The honour'd gashes whole.
>   [*To Scarus*] Give me thy hand.—
> To make this great fairy I'll commend thy acts,
> Make her thanks bless thee. [*To Cleo.*] O thou day o'th' world,
> Chain mine arm'd neck! Leap thou, attire and all,
> Through proof of harness to my heart, and there
> Ride on the pants triumphing!   (IV.viii.1–16)

We are a long way now from King Henry V's speech to his army at Harfleur, which came before the battle to inspire his troops rather than afterward to thank them, which asked them to "show us here/ The mettle of your pasture," as if they were cows, not Hectors, and which finally asked them to serve the cause of "Harry, England, and St. George." For Antony, nobody has served another's cause. Each man has made the public issue personal, and this fusion is projected into the future: a battle in which men have achieved their separate wholeness can leave no scars, and it takes only tears and kisses to restore health all round. Gashes are doubly honored when they are kissed whole. This equation between kisses and gashes, love and honor, culminates in Antony's final lines to Cleopatra. In the morning he had called her the armorer of his heart; now he invites her to achieve by her love what no man could do with a sword, to penetrate his armor and reach his heart, and yet not to displace the armor but to merge with it, and thus "ride on the pants triumphing." In that fabulous image Antony encompasses his whole range of experience and aspiration. Its obscenity reflects accurately one ingredient of his relation with Cleopatra, which must finally justify his approaching ruin. But its obscenity also becomes part of its exuberance, part of that enlargement by which naked privacy becomes a sign of public health and Antony's several parts of life are fused. For this moment Antony has made good in the world his greatest aspirations; he has become God's spy in the battle itself, not looking down from a protected viewpoint. This completes a process by which he has managed not to reject the world in its stale practice but to consume it, to use up and incarnate all its positive values. The seemingly erratic vacillations of conduct by which he moved back and forth from Egypt to Rome without denying either, and the suffering and self-reproval attendant upon that process, have enlarged him to a point where he is able to contain those public and private loyalties that were formerly opposed. He has achieved in his life, though only momentarily, the equation of love and honor, and he is ready to depart from the world leaving nothing wasted. He has earned the right to emerge on a plane of existence where "souls do couch on flowers," which does not compensate his loss of the world but reflects his absolute mastery of life. On the morning after his victory on land, Antony himself announces this emergence in a line deeply prophetic of Cleopatra's later symbolic transformation. Going forth to the battle that will end in his defeat and death, he is already no longer a man but a spirit, ready not to give up the world but to fight for it in and through the very elements of which it is made:

> I would they'ld fight i' th' fire or i' th' air;
> We'ld fight there too.   (IV.x.3-4)

II

The grand climax of the whole action is reserved for Cleopatra, who now learns the lesson of Antony's life, gives up her one-sided effort to bend the public world to her narrow purposes, and by her loyalty to him confirms Antony's achieved balance of public and private values. Until Actium, Cleopatra has tried to beguile Antony from his Roman thoughts and, in the process, has devoted her main energy to self-consciously primping herself up into an attractively elusive mistress. But with the defeat at Actium she begins to learn that the Roman honor that Antony now serves can never again be dismissed, evaded, or undermined. She has depended upon Antony either to ignore his public commitments in order to prove the measure of his love, as he was ready to do in the first scene of the play, or else to perform them in the perfunctory fashion of one who keeps his heart uncaught by the world and thus keeps himself worthy of her love. Much to her surprise, her expectations are continuously disappointed: Antony now insists upon a more rigorously defined honor than he had first gone to Rome to renew. That is why he is so violent in railing at himself and her, and Cleopatra is shocked and unprepared for his intensity. She recognizes after Actium that the elaborate stratagems by which she handled him earlier in the play can no longer be effective, but she does not know what alternatives to pursue, and she—Cleopatra!—is left speechless and nonplussed. She resorts to fragmentary, stuttering, disingenuous attempts to placate Antony and fend him off until she can gauge his mood and learn to respond accordingly. From the time of Actium until Antony's death, almost all of Cleopatra's speeches are attempts to defend herself against Antony's railing or to rein-

state herself in his pleasure, and most of them are little tongue-
tied half- and one-line affairs designed to parry Antony while
she regroups her wits:

> O, my pardon!   (III.xi.61)
>
> That head, my lord? (III.xiii.19)
>
> Good my lord—   (III.xiii.109)
>
> I must stay his time.   (III.xiii.155)
>
> That's my brave lord!   (III.xiii.177)
>
> Call all his noble captains to my lord.   (III.xiii.189)
>
> [*aside to Eno.*] What means this?   (IV.ii.13)
>
> Is not this buckled well?   (IV.iv.11)
>
> Why is my lord enrag'd against his love?   (IV.xii.31)

It takes Antony's death to make her understand that he has
passed as far beyond her Egyptian wiles as beyond the Roman
reason of the unreconstructed Enobarbus; and even then, she
only perceives the significance of Antony's final suffering and
glory by having to re-enact it herself. Antony must be cleared
out of the way, so to speak, before Cleopatra can recover her
balance and her voice, for Antony, in his effort to connect his
public and private interests, has in fact been protecting Cleopatra
from any need to face the problem. Antony has been her buffer,
and, in the paradoxical manner characteristic of tragedy, the
price of Cleopatra's self-centeredness has been Antony's painful
growth. Once Antony is dying, Cleopatra recovers her voice,
and almost from her first words it is clear that she is approaching Antony's final vision. Having tricked Antony into killing
himself by resorting to her old wiliness, she emerges with her
faith in that wiliness fatally shattered and is on her way to
becoming finally the lass unparalleled of her monument. When
Antony is hoisted aloft to die in her arms, we see a new
Cleopatra:

> *Ant.*   I am dying, Egypt, dying.
> Give me some wine, and let me speak a little.

Cleo. No, let me speak; and let me rail so high
That the false huswife Fortune break her wheel,
Provok'd by my offence.

Ant. One word, sweet queen.
Of Caesar seek your honour, with your safety. O!

Cleo. They do not go together.

Ant. Gentle, hear me.
None about Caesar trust but Proculeius.

Cleo. My resolution and my hands I'll trust;
None about Caesar. (IV.xv.41–50)

She admits for the first time that she has committed an offense, about which she refuses to deceive herself now that it has cost her that love which all her strategy was intended to secure. Where Antony had momentarily blamed his decline upon Fortune's wheel, Cleopatra immediately, if indirectly, recognizes a causal connection between her offense and the wheel's turning. Above all, she now rejects a means of safety that is inconsistent with her honor, exhibiting for the first time a capacity to transcend, if only as yet verbally, the self-centeredness that has been her mainspring of conduct.

Of course, Cleopatra does not now discard her old cunning like an outworn garment. Until the very end she continues to bargain with Caesar for her safety, perhaps with greater subtlety than we have seen in her so far. But there is a new dimension to her strategy, which is not merely verbal. After Antony's death she is no longer willing to secure her safety at any price, and her negotiations with Caesar are designed to test how far her safety and her honor may in fact go together. She reserves an area of maneuver that cannot be reached by considerations of personal security. Her bid for safety is increasingly controlled by her loyalty to Antony's memory. Instead of becoming just another item in her list of sexual triumphs, like Pompey and Julius Caesar, Antony now becomes the very condition of her further existence; she is willing to bargain for her safety only if in spirit she can keep giving herself to him. Just as Antony had been able to announce simultaneously yet without contradiction his intention to do all by the rule with Octavia and still to return to Egypt, so Cleopatra now achieves the moral elevation of discontinuity and is able to bargain with Caesar without betraying Antony.

We see her perform this magnificent feat mainly in her negotiations with Proculeius and Dolabella. First, Shakespeare shows us, out of Cleopatra's view, that Proculeius is another of Caesar's lackeys, wholly undeserving of the trust that Antony urged her to repose in him. This information not only arouses our anxiety for the outcome of Cleopatra's interview with Proculeius, but it enables us to maintain a detached and critical perspective upon Cleopatra. The odds are stacked against her in such a way that she will be doubly tempted to compromise herself and betray Antony's memory, and yet be all the more noble if she withstands the temptation. The interview with Proculeius, especially as it has been anticipated by the similar negotiation with Thyreus after Actium, becomes a crucial test of Cleopatra's integrity, and she passes it with incredible skill. Just as Shakespeare has given us crucial information about Proculeius out of Cleopatra's hearing, so he has Cleopatra voice her mood before Proculeius confronts her:

> My desolation does begin to make
> A better life. 'Tis paltry to be Caesar.
> Not being Fortune, he's but Fortune's knave,
> A minister of her will. And it is great
> To do that thing that ends all other deeds,
> Which shackles accidents and bolts up change,
> Which sleeps, and never palates more the dung,
> The beggar's nurse and Caesar's.   (V.ii.1-8)

Clearly this wins our approval. Her contempt for Caesar and her meditation upon suicide show her ready to forego her old wiliness and submit her personal interests to a higher discipline. Then Proculeius invites her "sweet dependency" upon Caesar, and she replies:

> Pray you tell him
> I am his fortune's vassal and I send him
> The greatness he has got. I hourly learn
> A doctrine of obedience, and would gladly
> Look him i' th' face.   (V.ii.28–32)

To read this speech in isolation is necessarily to conclude that Cleopatra is up to her old tricks and has remained unaffected by the death of Antony. But even Proculeius is not so short-sighted: he surprises and disarms Cleopatra, preventing her first attempt at the suicide foretold by her preceding speech. Read as it must be in the light of that earlier speech, Cleopatra's speech to Proculeius is heavily ironic and full of the most carefully premeditated ambiguities. Cleopatra calls herself the "vassal" of Caesar's fortune, but she has just called him "Fortune's knave,/ A minister of her will," so that her own slavery is equaled by his. She now sends him nigglingly "The greatness he has got," which she has already described as "paltry." And her "doctrine of obedience" involves simultaneously her submission to Caesar's political power and to Antony's example of suicide.

When Dolabella comes to second Proculeius' efforts, Cleopatra's transformation has markedly progressed. She has a new certainty, a confidence in her intentions, which emboldens her to discard the protective device of ambiguous utterance and uses her most elaborate and impassioned eulogy for her dead lover in order to pry Caesar's secret from Dolabella. He is suave at first and even a little flirtatious, as if hoping like Thyreus for a hand to kiss:

Dol.   Most noble Empress, you have heard of me?

Cleo.   I cannot tell.

Dol.   Assuredly you know me.

> (V.ii.71–72)

But instead of playing games with Dolabella, Cleopatra breaks over his repeated half-line protests to tell him her dream of Antony. What fills her mind now is that magnanimity of spirit which Antony achieved before his death, and which Cleopatra did not understand in the banquet scene:

> For his bounty,
> There was no winter in't; an autumn 'twas
> That grew the more by reaping. His delights
> Were dolphin-like: they show'd his back above
> The element they liv'd in. In his livery
> Walk'd crowns and crownets. Realms and islands were
> As plates dropp'd from his pocket.   (V.ii.86–92)

With this speech, which makes Antony's transfiguration the occasion for that of Cleopatra, she bewitches and enthralls Dolabella, who can only respond with "Cleopatra!" The result, to be sure, is that she pries from him the secret of Caesar's intention to lead her through Rome in triumph. But it makes all the difference that now she accomplishes this strategic end by what for her are the wholly improbable means of denying the blandishments of Dolabella and of refusing to indulge in her old duplicity.

We can measure the change in Cleopatra by comparing her response to Dolabella with her earlier response to Thyreus when he represented Caesar on a similar mission after Antony's defeat at Actium. With none of Dolabella's indirection, Thyreus had asked to kiss her hand in Caesar's name, and Cleopatra replied:

> Your Caesar's father oft,
> When he hath mus'd of taking kingdoms in,
> Bestow'd his lips on that unworthy place
> As it rain'd kisses.   (III.xiii.83–86)

There was nothing absolutely disloyal to Antony in this; and when Antony raged at her for flirting with Thyreus, she was right to reply, "Not know me yet?". For she had made the same offer of her "bluest veins to kiss; a hand that kings/ Have lipp'd, and trembled kissing" to her own messenger from Rome in return for good news of Antony; and Antony himself was to request her hand for Scarus to kiss after the land battle. Passing her hands around to be kissed, like hopping forty paces through the street, was one of Cleopatra's ways of maintaining that Egyptian value for which Antony was ready to live and die. But surely there was something disingenuous in a reply to Thyreus that managed to allude to Julius Caesar and keep strictly silent about her present lover Antony. Now with Dolabella she is unwilling to keep silent about Antony, and she is no longer concerned with making a public show of herself in hand-kissing. It was foreseeable that with Proculeius and Dolabella she might repeat the earlier maneuver with Thyreus. Instead, she discovers in herself what she had not been able to demonstrate before, the full depth and range of her passion for Antony, and this new clarity liberates her from her old wiliness. She has come finally to the point of disciplining her volatile private desires by honorable public commitments, and these public loyalties are thrust upon her by the intensity of her personal feelings. In Cleopatra as in Antony—and just because of Antony—the divergent aspects of life are being submitted to each other.

Cleopatra goes on bargaining with Caesar until the very end, reserving part of her treasure (until betrayed by her treasurer Seleucus), and continually probing to see whether she will be led through Rome in triumph. But here, too, she is following Antony, in *refusing to choose* between her safety and her honor. In her concern for safety, and especially in the importance she attaches to being humiliated in Caesar's triumph, we see the old Cleopatra still intact, unable to tolerate anything less than the universal gaze formerly bestowed upon the burnished throne at Cydnus. But she has also been a creature of infinite variety. If she cannot now maintain her identity and yet submit herself to a wagon ride through jeering Rome, that is because a value beyond variety has become necessary to her. She was piqued at the beginning to discover in Antony that a Roman thought had struck him; but now she strives toward a constancy that will enable her to act according to what she calls the "high Roman fashion." Cleopatra's wiliness at the end of the play is directed not at ingratiating herself with Caesar by flattery but at frustrating him by preserving a means to escape being led in triumph through the streets. When it becomes clear that her safety and her honor no longer can go together, when the world proves no more hospitable to her aspirations than it had been to Antony's, it turns out that she has used her cunning to prepare for the event. She has not merely used Dolabella to discover Caesar's plans for her and arranged to have the asps smuggled into her monument. In dealing with Caesar and his factors she has preserved her loyalty to Antony in such a fashion that her suicide can be a morally coherent event, the logical culmination of her life rather than an erratic, impulsive effort merely to rob death of its sting or to avoid embarrassment at Rome. Like Antony's, her suicide becomes a merging of safety and honor, private and public values. She has re-enacted Antony's experience, and thus has earned the right to platonize her aspirations and transform herself from a triple-turned whore into a true wife:

> Husband, I come!
> Now to that name my courage prove my title!
> I am fire and air; my other elements
> I give to baser life.   (V.ii.290–93)

III

When Cleopatra applies the asp to her breast, she says she wishes she could hear it speak and call Caesar "ass,/ Unpolicied!" She had said of Caesar earlier that not being Fortune, he was but a minister of Fortune's will. On the Roman side there has been from the beginning the same intimate connection between the belief in Fortune and the belief in policy—or "vantage"—that characterized Shakespeare's Machiavels in the earlier plays. The word "Fortune" is highly prominent in *Antony and Cleopatra,* and always in Roman mouths it means either unruly chance or fixed destiny. Early in the play, Maecenas says that Octavia will be a "blessed lottery" to Antony; near the end, Caesar tells Cleopatra that the injuries she has done to him he will remember only "As things done by chance." When Caesar greets his sister after Antony has returned to Egypt, he says, "let determined things to destiny/ Hold unbewail'd their way"; and in his great speech upon the death of Antony he laments "that our stars,/ Unreconcilable, should divide/ Our equalness to this." Now the belief in chance and the belief in fate are surely incompatible in some respects, but they have this in common: both deny man's unaided power to shape himself and his world in morally stable and coherent forms. In *Antony and Cleopatra* Shakespeare makes the agent of political order, Octavius Caesar, also the symbol of this nihilism. The policy in pursuit of fortune that was attributed to the antagonists of order in *King Lear* is transferred to the preservers of order in *Antony and Cleopatra*. Then this policy itself is platonized and made an instrument of destiny. By making policy the medium of order, and by making the permanence of order an effect of destiny, Shakespeare irrevocably demotes the ideal of order from the high place it occupied in his earlier dramatic thought. He takes the last step in transforming that ideal from the *raison d'être* to the mere *donnée* of human action.

That is why, in *Antony and Cleopatra,* the outfacing of a "Fortune" that has become "true" instead of "false," because it is destined in any case to restore the order of the state, is no longer a static holding action on behalf of traditional forms of value. It has become a revolutionary act that creates new value in the world. Antony uses the word "fortune" as often as anybody in the play, but he uses it characteristically in the plural, as when he says that he once made and marred men's "fortunes" (as if it did not matter which, so irrelevant are "fortunes"), or when he reminds Cleopatra of his former "fortunes" as the greatest prince of the world. He is not required, as Cordelia is, to face down an external power that threatens destruction to his world. Cordelia, whose whole character is encompassed in her granitic stability, needs to stand fast in order to draw the sting from fortune. But in Antony's fortunate public world, the threatened harm is Antony's internal failure to be his own variegated self and keep transforming into each other a required public steadfastness and a gratuitous private magnanimity. Antony needs continually to affirm the best that is in him both of Egypt and Rome. So long as he has both the clarity to maintain his embattled adherence to his Roman honor and the generosity to change places with his servants, he draws the sting from his failed fortunes by accepting them as necessary conditions of life and going on from there. By this acceptance Antony is able to outrun the world's flaws and to "become" his own, and thereby to win new honor for human life. He is able to create his place in a morally coherent universe without relying upon destiny and without the help of that shaping providence which vindicated Cordelia.

To affirm that providence, the play of *King Lear* had to end with the gratuitous deaths of Lear and Cordelia, which are no doubt the greatest example in Shakespeare of what we call "tragic waste." Much of the pain we feel at the end of *King Lear* comes from the enormous disproportion between the catastrophe itself and the comparatively slight mistake that activated those forces that in turn made the catastrophe necessary. But in the world beyond providence of *Antony and Cleopatra* there is no tragic waste. The lovers' lives have been gratuitous and self-defining, and therefore death comes full of reconcilation, bringing an increment of existence rather than a diminution. Death confers an earned immortality. Lear has suffered so much that we are ready to accept, with whatever regret, Kent's admonition "Vex not his ghost," and let him die; the truth affirmed by *King Lear* does barely enable us to accept the death of Cordelia. But for Antony and Cleopatra we do not accept death but desire it, as Cleopatra says, like a lover's pinch. For them life has reached that brimful level where, as Antony says finally, "Now all labour/ Mars what it does: yea, very force entangles/ Itself with strength"; and therefore, as Cleopatra says to the asp, "Come, thou mortal wretch,/ With thy sharp teeth this knot intrinsicate/ Of life at once untie." Life has been completed, used up; like the patriarchs of the Old

Testament, these lovers, whatever their age, are full of days. They are faced toward an immortal life that Antony imagines in highly specific terms:

> Where souls do couch on flowers, we'll hand in hand
> And with our sprightly port make the ghosts gaze.
> Dido and her Aeneas shall want troops,
> And all the haunt be ours.   (IV.xiv.51–54)

Here the ghosts are anything but vexed, and the lovers are again the objects of an admiration so universal that, like Cleopatra at Cydnus, it all but causes a gap in nature. Cleopatra's final vision marvellously complements this of Antony's, by connecting death with the beginning of life in an image of motherhood and nurture:

> Peace, peace!
> Dost thou not see my baby at my breast,
> That sucks the nurse asleep?   (V.ii.311–13)

In transforming Cleopatra's whoredom into greatness, Shakespeare makes her first the wife of Antony and then the gentle mother of that death which will reunite her with her husband where souls do couch on flowers. Everything surrounding the lovers' deaths—the voluntariness of their suicides, the supporting suicides of their servants, and the awed choric comments even of Octavius, " . . . she looks like sleep,/ As she would catch another Antony/ In her strong toil of grace"—serves to transform death itself into a symbolic renewal of existence on the level of those aspirations that motivated the lovers' discontinuous conduct in the play.

I will be concerned in the next chapter with the way in which the style of the play shapes and reflects the whole process of the action as I have described it, and especially as that action culminates in the transfiguration of death. Here it remains to be said that the play's symbolic treatment of death as apotheosis, poised against the usual dramatic significance of death as catastrophe, marks an important place in Shakespeare's development. It looks backward to *King Lear* and *Macbeth* in that Shakespeare is not yet willing to lighten the weight of suffering and death as the price of human frailty and therefore of life itself. Yet he has outgrown the earlier conception of death as the avenging instrument of a providential order, for he has discovered in life an element of reconciliation that cannot be rendered in a naturalistic treatment of death. His symbolic treatment of that powerful force in the final speeches of *Antony and Cleopatra* looks forward to *Cymbeline, The Winter's Tale,* and *The Tempest,* plays on the theme of reconciliation that are uniformly symbolic in method. But where we may sometimes feel in those last plays that Shakespeare's symbolic technique lightly veils the actual boundaries of life in order to avoid the inescapable significance of death, in *Antony and Cleopatra* his willingness to face up to death leaves no such evasive impression. *Antony and Cleopatra* encompasses both the naturalism of death in *King Lear* and the symbolism of reconciliation in *The Tempest.* That is why, in this play alone among Shakespeare's works, death itself is exuberant. And that in turn is why *Antony and Cleopatra* may be placed alongside *King Lear* and *The Tempest* as one of Shakespeare's supreme masterpieces.

CHAPTER SIX

THE PROTEAN LANGUAGE OF
THE MAN-MADE WORLD

F INALLY, I come to the style of the play, which might properly have a book to itself. Ever since Coleridge's dictum, that "*feliciter audax* is the motto for its style comparatively with [Shakespeare's] other works, even as it is the general motto for all his works compared with other poets," [1] this style has been widely admired, even by those who find in the play an unrelieved record of dissoluteness and corruption. But the style of *Antony and Cleopatra* is nothing less than the whole *Gestalt* of the play—the story as it is crystallized out of the welter of materials in Plutarch, its unique sequence of episodes, irrespective of their individual linguistic features, and the changes wrought during the play in the quality of language and action. In this pattern the verbal texture is only a single element; and now we must consider the language, not in every facet of its lush magificence, as if it were the play itself, but only in so far as it helps to create and reflect the total pattern in which it participates.

That pattern, I have suggested, embodies the transfiguration of life, a process in which the uses of this world are purified and projected freshly in their dynamic essences rather than left behind to become stale and flat. In speaking of the platonizing of the lovers' experience, or of their emergence in a transcendental realm, I have not had in mind a mystical meaning beyond the power of words to convey.[2] The power of language in *Antony and Cleopatra* is just that it makes palpable this cosmic realm. All the principal features of the language—the vastness of the imagery, the sublimated abstractness of the diction, the discontinuity of broken syntax in language relating to the person, and the syntactical flow of language that describes the world—all serve to show that the characters are creating by their action a new, coherent, and protean life that guarantees man's moral freedom and his power to create endlessly a unique identity.

The most striking quality of the imagery is what the late S. L. Bethell called its Brobdingnagian vastness. The characters are given mythic size, and their actions universal importance, by the hyperbole of the language. Antony is repeatedly called a pillar of the world; he in turn keeps addressing Cleopatra as "Egypt." He will let Rome melt for her sake, and she will unpeople Egypt for his. When Maecenas asks Enobarbus to verify the rumor that in Egypt they had eight wild boars roasted whole at a breakfast for twelve persons, Enobarbus replies, "This was as a fly by an eagle. . . . " The boundaries of Rome are called the sides of the world, and the bounty of Antony is called an autumn, as if the seasons, like the kings of Cappadocia and Paphlagonia, were his lieutenants. When Cleopatra appeared in her barge at Cydnus, Enobarbus tells us, there was a gap in nature; and when Antony dies, Cleopatra tells us, the crown of the earth does melt, and our lamp is spent. Again and again the lovers are compared with mythological figures, with the sun and the moon, and with light itself; and these comparisons have no regard for the fixed categories of the traditional doctrine of correspondences. They are eclectic, even sometimes blasphemous, from the point of view of a hierarchically ordered world that might provide the basis for any consistent language of analogy. They show another kind of world, and yet they are not specious nor merely decorative comparisons; they dignify the characters spatially because they are credible in the light of the characters' thought and action in the play.

Closely related in function and effect to this imagery of vastness is a high degree of abstraction in the diction, reinforced by the extreme indirection of the syntax, which serves to transform the lovers' transitory earthly experience into permanent conceptual meaning without negating its source in flesh. A good example of this technique is Philo's opening speech of the play:

> Nay, but this dotage of our general's
> O'erflows the measure. Those his goodly eyes
> That o'er the files and musters of the war
> Have glow'd like plated Mars, now bend, now turn
> The office and devotion of their view
> Upon a tawny front. His captain's heart,
> Which in the scuffles of great fights hath burst
> The buckles on his breast, reneges all temper
> And is become the bellows and the fan
> To cool a gypsy's lust.   (I.i.1-10)

Almost all the nouns and adjectives, until the last two lines, are highly abstract, generalized, and non-sensory. Antony is not directly named, and he is not permitted to engage syntactically in the action described: his dotage and his eyes and his heart take the verbs and perform his action for him. That action has the disembodied quality of a perpetual motion. It is not Antony but his eyes that view Cleopatra, and even then not directly: between the eyes and their presumably base object is interposed "the office and devotion of their view," a highly honorific function that is controlled not by a single gesture but in the apparently endless alternation of bending and turning. If the office of eyes is to perform a perpetual devotion, then the object of their view must be reverential; and the suitably abstract and enticing "tawny front" allows us to conceive of Cleopatra as such an object. (Even later in the play, when Antony rails his worst at her, he calls Cleopatra by similarly sublimated names: "A fragment of Gnaeus Pompey's," "false soul," "right gipsy," and "the greatest spot of all thy sex.") The effect of the diction is to purify the conduct described of the sullied flesh that is its medium; the effect of the syntax is to remove and cleanse Antony from the moral taint of that conduct. Thus at the end of the first scene, when Antony's behavior has confirmed Philo's judgment before our eyes, and Demetrius says,

> I am full sorry
> That he approves the common liar, who
> Thus speaks of him at Rome. . . .   (I.i.59-61)

that single word "liar" takes back all that the rest concedes, and, paradoxically, we are invited to believe both that Antony is in his dotage and that anybody who says so is a liar.

This stylistic technique is pervasive in the play, and it comes to serve a broader purpose than insulating Antony (and Cleopatra) from such adverse judgments as that of Philo's speech. It transforms the conduct that it describes into an archetypal value by imparting to it an integrity that transcends personal judgments. By the use of metonymy, inversion, infinitive phrases, and passive constructions, the style keeps subordinating the persons to their actions, which are then universalized by the abstractness of the diction. The characters turn up syntactically only as the objects of verbs and prepositions, and as the subjects of the subordinate clauses; they are made to seem the impersonal media through which cosmic forces work on the world:

> You are too indulgent. Let us grant it is not
> Amiss to tumble on the bed of Ptolemy,
> To give a kingdom for a mirth, to sit
> And keep the turn of tippling with a slave,
> To reel the streets at noon, and stand the buffet
> With knaves that smell of sweat. . . .
>
>   . . . But to confound such time
> That drums him from his sport and speaks as loud
> As his own state and ours—'tis to be chid
> As we rate boys who, being mature in knowledge,
> Pawn their experience to their present pleasure
> And so rebel to judgment.   (I.iv.16–33)
>
>   What though you fled
> From that great face of war whose several ranges
> Frighted each other? why should he follow?
> The itch of his affection should not then
> Have nick'd his captainship, at such a point,
> When half to half the world oppos'd, he being
> The meered question. 'Twas a shame no less
> Than was his loss, to course your flying flags
> And leave his navy gazing.   (III.xiii.4–12)
>
>   Eros,
> Wouldst thou be window'd in great Rome and see
> Thy master thus with pleach'd arms, bending down
> His corrigible neck, his face subdu'd

> To penetrative shame, whilst the wheel'd seat
> Of fortunate Caesar, drawn before him, branded
> His baseness that ensu'd?   (IV.xiv.71–77)

> Sir, I will eat no meat, I'll not drink, sir;
> If idle talk will once be necessary,
> I'll not sleep neither. This mortal house I'll ruin,
> Do Caesar what he can. Know, sir, that I
> Will not wait pinion'd at your master's court
> Nor once be chastis'd with the sober eye
> Of dull Octavia. Shall they hoist me up
> And show me to the shouting varletry
> Of censuring Rome? Rather a ditch in Egypt
> Be gentle grave unto me! Rather on Nilus' mud
> Lay me stark-nak'd, and let the waterflies
> Blow me into abhorring! Rather make
> My country's high pyramides my gibbet
> And hang me up in chains!   (V.ii.49–62)

Even these passages ostensibly damning the lovers serve to exalt them. Just as Antony fears that his face will be subdued to shame, so the characters are repeatedly subdued to those qualities and actions that, like Rome, are the independent moving parts of the world embodied in the style. Reputation, shame, captainship, and baseness, along with all the conduct incarnated in infinitive phrases, constitute the agents of action. Hence it is not surprising that in this play the word *become,* in the sense of *fitting,* is frequently used to relate individual persons to these large conceptual agencies:

> Look, prithee, Charmian,
> How this Herculean Roman does become
> The carriage of his chafe.   (I.iii.83–85)

> But, sir, forgive me;
> Since my becomings kill me when they do not
> Eye well to you. . . .   (I.iii.95–97)

> . . . for vilest things
> Become themselves in her, that the holy priests
> Bless her when she is riggish.   (II.ii.243–45)

> Observe how Antony becomes his flaw,
> And what thou think'st his very action speaks
> In every power that moves.   (III.xii.34–36)

This abstract and sublimated style fittingly stands in the sharpest contrast to the highly concrete style of *King Lear*. There the syntax is straightforward, and the diction is specific and sensory. The intellectual concern of *King Lear* is with the ultimate basis of our moral categories and conduct, and one way in which the play gets down to fundamentals is in the almost physical directness of its style. In Lear's curses upon his daughters and in his madness, we would normally expect a high degree of concreteness. But in fact we find this concrete diction to be the medium of patient as well as impatient thought throughout the play, in Edmund's Machiavellian soliloquies, in Edgar's account of his father's death, or in Lear's discourse in the storm before he goes mad:

> Thou think'st 'tis much this contentious storm
> Invades us to the skin. So 'tis to thee;
> But where the greater malady is fix'd,
> The lesser is scarce felt. Thou 'dst shun a bear;
> But if thy flight lay toward the raging sea,
> Thou 'dst meet the bear i' th' mouth. When the mind's free,
> The body's delicate. The tempest in my mind
> Doth from my senses take all feeling else
> Save what beats there. Filial ingratitude!
> Is it not as this mouth should tear this hand
> For lifting food to 't? But I will punish home!
> No, I will weep no more. In such a night
> To shut me out! Pour on; I will endure. (III.iv.6–18)

These speeches characteristically begin with the abstraction, and then move to pin it down by concrete images. But the images are typically so vivid and direct, like the references here to the encounter with the bear and to the mouth tearing the hand that feeds it, that they make us lose the train of abstract thought and leave us adrift amidst the unsorted shapes of the physical world. The style keeps undermining abstract categories of thought, reflecting and universalizing the progressive collapse of Lear's mind, and justifying the play's ultimate concern with the basis in nature for human morality. As against this movement of the style downward into concreteness in *King Lear,* the movement in *Antony and Cleopatra* is upward into abstraction, and yet a form of abstraction that does not obliterate the physical. We can see the difference by comparing Lear's "Is it not as this mouth should tear this hand/ For lifting food to 't?" with Cleopatra's "let the water-flies/ Blow me into abhorring." In fact, Cleopatra is also talking about the eating of her own flesh, and she has begun concretely enough by her reference to the Nile's mud and its water-flies; but when she comes to name the deed, she glances off into an image that is conceptual rather than sensory. The movement of the diction from "water-flies" to "blow" to "abhorring" sublimates the physical without denying it; and by this process of its style, *Antony and Cleopatra* keeps hallowing even the most unseemly details of physical life. In this style is wrought the suggestion of immortality that is the play's unique achievement, and its special contribution to Shakespeare's development.

II

It is also possible to distinguish two opposite rhythms made by the syntax, and to suggest a thematic basis for this distinction. On the one hand, there is an extreme abruptness of movement, a jerky discontinuity from phrase to phrase and sentence to sentence, which is produced largely by the syntactical indirections I have described and which serves to isolate consecutive statements, and consecutive speakers, from one another. On the other hand, there are long and flowing movements, beautifully integrated by their rhythms, uniting separate statements, carrying forward from speaker to speaker, and continuously binding up wholes that are greater than the sums of their parts. Here are two pairs of passages, the first illustrating the difference through individual speeches, the second showing the contrasting rhythms in consecutive speeches:

> Off, pluck off!
> The sevenfold shield of Ajax cannot keep
> The battery from my heart. O, cleave, my sides!
> Heart, once be stronger than thy continent,

Crack thy frail case! Apace, Eros, apace.—
No more a soldier. Bruised pieces, go;
You have been nobly borne.—From me awhile.
I will o'ertake thee, Cleopatra, and
Weep for my pardon. So it must be, for now
All length is torture. Since the torch is out,
Lie down, and stray no farther. Now all labour
Mars what it does; yea, very force entangles
Itself with strength. Seal then, and all is done.
Eros!—I come, my queen.—Eros!—Stay for me.
Where souls do couch on flowers, we'll hand in hand
And with our sprightly port make the ghosts gaze.
Dido and her Aeneas shall want troops,
And all the haunt be ours.—Come, Eros, Eros!

(IV.xiv.37–54)

Nay, pray you seek no colour for your going,
But bid farewell, and go. When you su'd staying,
Then was the time for words. No going then!
Eternity was in our lips and eyes,
Bliss in our brows' bent, none our parts so poor
But was a race of heaven. They are so still,
Or thou, the greatest soldier of the world,
Art turn'd the greatest liar.

(I.iii.32–39)

Eros.	Nay, gentle madam, to him! comfort him!
Iras.	Do, most dear Queen.
Char.	Do? Why, what else?
Cleo.	Let me sit down. O Juno!
Ant.	No, no, no, no, no!
Eros.	See you here, sir?
Ant.	O fie, fie, fie!
Char.	Madam!
Iras.	Madam, O good Empress!
Eros.	Sir, sir!
Ant.	Yes, my lord, yes! He at Philippi kept

His sword e'en like a dancer, while I struck
The lean and wrinkled Cassius; and 'twas I
That the mad Brutus ended.

(III.xi.25–37)

Cleo.	Have you done yet?
Ant.	Alack, our terrene moon Is now eclips'd, and it portends alone The fall of Antony!
Cleo.	I must stay his time.
Ant.	To flatter Caesar, would you mingle eyes With one that ties his points?
Cleo.	Not know me yet?
Ant.	Cold-hearted toward me?
Cleo.	Ah, dear, if I be so, From my cold heart let heaven engender hail, And poison it in the source. . . .

(III.xiii.153–160)

Whether one favors light or heavy pointing of the text, there is nevertheless a striking contrast between the staccato-like abruptness of movement in the first passages in each pair, and the orchestrated continuity of movement in the second passages. Neither of these rhythms is used exclusively in a particular kind of situation or for a single thematic purpose. But there is certainly a characteristic use of the broken rhythm to depict the characters, especially Antony, in those moments both of deepest anguish and of highest fulfilment when they are most alone in the world. We find this rhythm in Antony's self-recrimination after the defeat at Actium, in his celebration of the land victory, and, as in the passage cited above, in his reception of the false news of Cleopatra's death. The discontinuous style is the mode in which he relates himself, "so lated in the world," to those large cosmic forces that impersonally make him their instrument; it is his way of encompassing both his virtue and his flaw. The discontinuous speech is an extension of that general discontinuity in action and characterization that I have described; it shows Antony first suffering and then transfiguring the two worlds of public and private values, without denying the integrity of either one.

The other rhythm, which keeps integrating musically the most disparate qualities, is conspicuous in passages where the characters speak of their relationships with one another, as in Cleopatra's speech cited above, or where they are describing each other, as in Enobarbus' famous description of Cleopatra's barge or Cleopatra's paeans to Antony after he is dead. Third-person discourse is necessarily more remote than first-person, and less susceptible to the broken immediacy of the individual character's negotiation with life. Here its large inclusive rhythms also provide a stabilizing framework for the staccato drift of the broken style. And in combination with those characteristics of the diction that I have described, the flowing rhythm serves to measure and articulate the transcendent realm of experience that is the final locus of the play's action. It helps to engender that platonized cosmic structure which now replaces the ordered hierarchies of the doctrine of correspondences in the earlier plays I have discussed.

In talking about the world made by the style in *Antony and Cleopatra*, it is impossible to separate the diction, imagery, syntax, and rhythm. All converge to persuade us of the existence of a cosmic realm that is coherent and yet fluid, seamless in its continuity despite the fragmented discontinuity of the human life that it incorporates, and protean in its capacity for enlargement. This world can best be defined by contrast to the world incorporated in the style of the history plays, where we began. In the familiar language of correspondences in those plays, the concrete imagery, the straightforward syntax, and the regulated rhythms present us with a series of fixed analogies among the various hierarchies of being—angels, men, fish, birds, and so on—with their corresponding systems of conduct.[3] In each category every member has his place, and it is the meaning and purpose of his existence to fulfil his place with conduct proper to his kind. The ethical business of King Richard and Prince Hal is to earn their identification by analogy with the estridge, the dolphin, the sun, and with God. They are to achieve their fullness of being by making their scheme of life on earth a riplica of the prior scheme laid down in heaven, by imitating on earth the heavenly categories, as Prince Hal indicates in his soliloquy:

> Yet herein will I imitate the sun,
> Who doth permit the base contagious clouds
> To smother up his beauty from the world,
> That, when he please again to be himself,
> Being wanted, he may be more wond'red at,
> By breaking through the foul and ugly mists
> Of vapours that did seem to strangle him.
>
> (*I Henry IV*, I.ii.221–27)

That imagery and syntax is characteristic of the history plays, and it makes a world of correspondences in which there is no immediate access from one category to another, no transcendence, but only earthly fulfilment for those who sustain the cosmic analogies each within his own hierarchy of being. Each man is challenged to embody in himself the accurate reflection of some immutable otherworldly category. Each is asked to make some particular word into flesh.

The final effect of the language and syntax in *Antony and Cleopatra* is almost the reverse of this. This style implies no foreordained heavenly scheme. Rather it keeps abstracting the stunning variety of human experience into a series of otherworldly categories, which are then linked together by the shaping power of the rhythm. Here the intense and dutiful feeling for "degree" is relaxed, to make room for an exuberant yet controlled affirmation of "plenitude." [4] Instead of imitating some prescribed otherworldly scheme, each man is now invited to make his own, to transmute his particular flesh into some perfect and original word. The presence of this cosmic world is pervasive in the play, and cannot be illustrated by single quotations. All the elements of style that I have mentioned help to give it substance. Here I should like to add a list of passages that imply in one way or another the protean continuity between a character's conduct and the readiness of the cosmos to conform its hospitable categories to these unique human achievements.

Again and again in the play, the characters worry about falling away from, not "bias of nature," some prior external category, but themselves, in all their internal definition:

I'll seem the fool I am not. Antony
Will be himself.

(I.i.42–43)

Sir, sometimes when he is not Antony
He comes too short of that great property
Which still should go with Antony.

(I.i.57–59)

                    I shall entreat him
To answer like himself. If Caesar move him,
Let Antony look over Caesar's head
And speak as loud as Mars. By Jupiter,
Were I the wearer of Antonius' beard,
I would not shav't to-day!

(II.ii.3–8)

Not he that himself is not so; which is Mark Antony. He will to
his Egyptian dish again. Then shall the sighs of Octavia blow the
fire up in Caesar, and, as I said before, that which is the strength
of their amity shall prove the immediate author of their variance.
Antony will use his affection where it is. He married but his
occasion here.

(II.vi.132–40)

                Strong Enobarb
Is weaker than the wine, and mine own tongue
Splits what it speaks. The wild disguise hath almost
Antick'd us all. What needs more words? Good night.
Good Antony, your hand.

(II.vii.127–31)

                Had our general
Been what he knew himself, it had gone well.

(III.x.26–27)

            Let that be left
Which leaves itself. To the seaside straightway!

(III.xi.19–20)

                    It is my birthday.
I had thought t' have held it poor; but since my lord
Is Antony again, I will be Cleopatra.

(III.xiii.185–87)

Already in these passages, the definition of the self is related to something beyond, to Mars or to "that great property"; and there is another group of passages in which that relationship becomes explicit. This includes the already cited references to Antony's becoming "the carriage of his chafe" and becoming his "flaw," as well as the following:

> Experience, manhood, honour, ne'er before
> Did violate so itself.
>
> (III.x.23-24)

> I have offended reputation—
> A most unnoble swerving.
>
> (III.xi.49-50)

> O love,
> That thou couldst see my wars to-day, and knew'st
> The royal occupation! Thou shouldst see
> A workman in't.
>
> (IV.iv.15-18)

> The death of Antony
> Is not a single doom; in the name lay
> A moiety of the world.
>
> (V.i.17-19)

Finally, there are passages that seem to delineate the empty cosmic categories waiting to be filled up by the achieved selfhood of the characters; passages that imply the existence of a platonic world beyond appearances, but a fluid, dynamic world, rather than a static set of fixed categories:

> Why, sir, give the gods a thankful sacrifice. When it pleaseth their deities to take the wife of a man from him, it shows to man the tailors of the earth; comforting therein, that when old robes are worn out, there are members to make new.
>
> (I.ii.167-72)

> You shall find there
> A man who is the abstract of all faults
> That all men follow.
>
> (I.iv.8-10)

> Every time
> Serves for the matter that is then born in't.
>
> (II.ii.9–10)

> To be call'd into a huge sphere and not to be seen to move in't, are the holes where eyes should be, which pitifully disaster the cheeks.
>
> (II.vii.16–19)

> *Ant.*   Be a child o' th' time.
> *Caes.*   Possess it; I'll make answer.
>
> (II.vii.105–6)

All these passages produce a considerable range and diversity of effects. They are far from exhibiting the consistency among themselves that is characteristic of the world made by the style in the history plays. But that is because the cosmic world they embody is so much less schematic than that of the earlier plays. If the common elements in these passages are less obvious, they are no less structural in the play than what are in fact the clichés of the earlier cosmic imagery. The pervasive implication here is that man does not imitate but generates the forms of otherworldly perfection. It is as if each man's qualities, when he is truly himself, are projected in idealized form upon a transcendental screen, so that the cosmos keeps incorporating the world, instead of the world imperfectly imitating the cosmos. By the conduct of his life each man tailors his otherworldly garments, whose names are "experience," "manhood," "reputation," and "honour," instead of "sun," dolphin," and "estridge." Each man is expected simply to be his own best self, and not to rend those garments which he himself has made.

Thus "that great property/ Which still should go with Antony" is nothing we might have anticipated by reading a political treatise listing the qualifications of a Renaissance king serving as God's steward in the world. In the history plays and *King Lear*, Shakespeare paid his full respects to all such kingly properties but found them inadequate to fulfil a completely human, and hence vulnerable, life in the world. The great property to which Antony aspires is simply the ability to wear his own beard and not shave it, to act out in the world those qualities of experience, manhood, and honor that are attributed to him because he had already acquired them and not because they are prescribed by a code. Antony and Lepidus have been "call'd into a huge sphere" by something more immediate and personal than the accidents of birth or of local politics. By their conduct they have made that sphere their own; and, once having done so, they must now move in it, and fill it up with themselves. In the history plays the histrionic self-deception of the protagonists is related to the existence of externally sanctioned roles to be played. But whereas those protagonists were *obligated* from without to perform their public roles, these Roman characters are *responsible* from within to be themselves and not to fall into either role-playing or its substitute, self-deception. Whereas it was incumbent upon the English hero to imitate the sun, the Roman must not let himself be antick'd by the wild disguise.

Just as the cosmic world of *Antony and Cleopatra* is flexible enough to afford each man a "huge sphere" that is truly his own, it also allows for a continuous reshaping of its own contours. If at any moment it asks of each man that he keep himself within himself, it recognizes that from moment to moment a man's accumulated experience may transform him, and project into the world a new ingredient of manhood. The act of self-creation, unlike that of conforming to a protoype, never ends; and its endless flux and movement are represented in the play by Antony's great cloud speech, which comes closer than any other passage to incorporating all the characteristic features of the style I have described:

> Sometime we see a cloud that's dragonish;
> A vapour sometime like a bear or lion,
> A tower'd citadel, a pendent rock,
> A forked mountain, or blue promontory
> With trees upon't that nod unto the world
> And mock our eyes with air. Thou hast seen these signs;
> They are black Vesper's pageants.

· · · · · · · · · · ·

That which is now a horse, even with a thought
The rack dislimns, and makes it indistinct
As water is in water.

.   .   .   .

My good knave Eros, now thy captain is
Even such a body. Here I am Antony;
Yet cannot hold this visible shape, my knave.
I made these wars for Egypt; and the Queen—
Whose heart I thought I had, for she had mine,
Which, whilst it was mine, had annex'd unto't
A million moe, now lost—she, Eros, has
Pack'd cards with Caesar and false-play'd my glory
Unto an enemy's triumph.
Nay, weep not, gentle Eros. There is left us
Ourselves to end ourselves.   (IV.xiv.2–22)

Here is a profoundly tragic sense of mutability, of the fickleness of Fortune and the fatal deceptiveness of life. The syntax
and rhythm of the last eleven lines, in which words, phrases,
and clauses are dislimned into one another, reflect the blurring
and instability of experience that lead naturally to the idea of
suicide. But there is another dimension of feeling communicated
in which the mutability of experience becomes a condition of
its vitality and deceptiveness and instability the signs of an
infinitely protean continuity of existence. In the world of Prince
Hal's soliloquy the sun stood still, temporarily obscured by
"base contagious clouds," waiting to be hitched to the doctrine
of correspondences. In Antony's world it is the clouds and not
the sun that give structure to life, not by standing still but
by their continuously changing shapes. The dissolving of one
"visible shape" into another becomes part of a progression
whose corporeal and transcendental elements are coextensive,
a progression in which the world may be transcended only
because it has not been rejected for the safety of Lear's prison
but rather has been accepted in all the perishability of its many
possible shapes. In this progression suicide is robbed of its sting;
it becomes an act of innocence, creative rather than destructive.
It is an inevitable moment in that continuing transformation
of Antony's visible shape, from "strumpet's fool" to "pillar of

the world" to "fire and air." All means of transformation, after all, are necessary to those who partake of immortality.

For the language goes as far as language can in creating for the characters that immortality which I attributed to them at the beginning of this book. The cosmic language I have described is a continuous outgrowth of the dramatic action, not a superimposed ideological blueprint. It is a conceptual realization, from moment to moment and from one pillar of the world to another, of the quality and progress of the lovers' experience. The style itself is an aspect of that process by which first Antony and then Cleopatra stop defining their experience by the fixed categories called Rome and Egypt, and begin to move back and forth in order to unify public and private values. Their ability to make this connection, to live their Egyptian life after the high Roman fashion, earns them transcendence, an ascent from "Nilus' slime" to the realms of fire and air. And it completes the unfinished business of *King Lear*. Mr. Danby claims that in *King Lear* Shakespeare delivers his final message that the Good Man must have a Good Society, that until society can become good, even the transfigured Lear must be protected from it.[5] But now I think Shakespeare enables us to see in Antony how man, in achieving whatever goodness lies within his portion, may simultaneously transcend and transfigure the Bad Society. By accepting his own and the world's imperfection, by refusing to hide from himself in self-deception or from the world behind walls, poor fork'd Antony is enabled to fly about with the goodness that is his unconfined and unprotected, sometimes shrinking into effeminacy and sometimes enlarging into magnanimity. Goodness, after all, has an infinite need to renew itself, whatever the risk; and it has an infinite capacity for changing its visible shape.

From the beginning of the play Antony has, of all the characters, the largest stock of experience, manhood, and honor; and yet, from the beginning we have a powerful feeling that only he among the characters is alone in spirit, endlessly beset and endlessly responsive to a deep feeling for the contingency of experience. He is tortured, vacillating, confused, unwittingly moving in his true direction. Yet he feels himself "so lated in the world" that he has lost his way, for his society offers him no room, no comfort, no coherent emblems of conduct marked upon its pillars. When he earns Octavia's love, she deserts him; when he earns that of Cleopatra, she betrays him. Every way he turns is blocked, until he feels himself "shot . . . into the abysm of hell," where he loses himself in order to find himself. When the ambiguities and instabilities of his experience have thrown him back upon his innermost self, he finds the power to generate that visible shape in which, if he must, he becomes his flaw. In that graceful shape he achieves for himself, and bequeaths to Cleopatra, a joyous exuberance, which transfigures death itself. His world has forced him to find himself; in rising to his occasion and becoming the generous author of himself, he nurtures and transcends his world.

THE TEMPEST

A LMOST ALL of the major subjects and themes that I have discussed in connection with earlier plays are brought together in *The Tempest*. This play encompasses the cycle of political rebellion and reconstruction, from the usurpation by Antonio of Prospero's office in Milan, to his proposal on the island that Sebastian similarly take violent means to supplant *his* brother, to Prospero's defense of the threatened Alonso, and finally to the drawing of a magic circle within which the traitors are forgiven, Prospero is restored to his dukedom, and the original order is re-established. In all this the play exhibits a benign providence, which originally brought Prospero and Miranda safely to the island, which now brings the others within reach of Prospero's magic, and of which that magic itself is an instrument. Prospero's white magic is distinguished from the black magic of Sycorax by the ethical control with which Prospero wields its divine power; and this requires him at a crucial moment to renounce magic by renouncing revenge, forgiving his malefactors, and acquiescing in the impotence of divine magic to prevail against either the ignorance of his slave or the malice of his brother. Caliban and Antonio remain outside the final ring of reconciliation, reminding us that life will always breed outrageous fortune to be suffered, growing out of man's persisting sensuality and his all too corruptible reason. But Prospero's decision that "the rarer action is/ In virtue than in vengeance" reminds us too that it is possible to transform "Fortune" into "fortunes" through forgiveness, and, in the discharge of Ariel and the return to Milan, through a supreme magnanimity. The highest reach of Prospero's ethic is to give up his island Utopia and his God-spying magic and to submit himself once more, in the perishable shape of his human frailty, to the uses of the world.

The play gives weight and momentum to this climactic action by its familiar series of parallelisms and antitheses all centered upon Caliban.[1] One incidental effect of these freshly conceived correspondences is to show the burgeoning multiplicity of human circumstance and the strong lines of difference among things ostensibly alike: Antonio's civilized, and Caliban's natural, treachery; Ferdinand's high service and Caliban's base servility. But their main function is to make Caliban the experimental measure of all values. Caliban is the "salvage and deformed slave" against whose darkness we may see better how the light of our civilized humanity shines out, especially in the love of Ferdinand and Miranda. But Shakespeare treats Caliban nevertheless with miraculous respect, and declines to make him the vehicle of any simple-minded antiprimitivism. For one thing, he has Prospero take upon himself the responsibility for Caliban: "this thing of darkness/ I acknowledge mine." And in the same breath Prospero makes Alonso, King of Naples, responsible for Caliban's civilized confederates in a conspiracy against order, justice, and truth: "Two of these fellows you/ Must know and own." The drunkenness of Stephano and Trinculo is hardly preferable to the all but gracious deformity of Caliban; and neither is the malice of Antonio. Early in the play, when Prospero tells Miranda his history, he defies her to suppose that the treacherous Antonio might be his own brother. Miranda, who has never spent a day at court, replies:

> I should sin
> To think but nobly of my grandmother.
> Good wombs have borne bad sons. (I.ii.118–20)

That knowledge which made Lear mad, Miranda possesses as a birthright; and she goes beyond Lear's knowledge, to the discontinuity of Antony's, by continuing to think nobly of her grandmother. Then at the end of the play, when Antonio stands mute and unrepentant, Caliban shows signs of amendment. He calls the Europeans "brave spirits indeed," echoing Miranda's famous words; and of Prospero, against whom he has been consistently rebellious, he now says, "How fine my master is!" When Prospero admonishes him to look for pardon, Caliban replies, "I'll be wise hereafter,/ And seek for grace." I do not think we are meant to see a transformation in Caliban, but only the possibility that he may not remain always unregenerate. It is almost as if now that Prospero has abjured his divine magic, Caliban may be relieved of the effects of that dark power that has thus far determined his life in the world. Meanwhile, it is Antonio in his silence who remains unregenerate.

In Antonio a good womb has borne a bad son, and in Caliban Prospero must acknowledge the thing of darkness his. Miranda nevertheless thinks nobly of her grandmother, and Prospero renounces revenge and abjures his magic. The "nature-civilization" contrast centered upon Caliban finally shows no consistent difference between the two conditions; it shows all life to be of one piece, constantly subject to the several kinds of darkness within man, but also susceptible to light through a voluntary discontinuous maganimity. In Prospero, Shakespeare writes his most artfully elaborate variation on the answer to Hamlet's question about the character of human life; and in the process he concedes the necessary impermanence of political order. Horatio, who in suffering all suffered nothing, was nevertheless a peripheral character without leverage upon events. Cordelia's ability to outface fortune had a decisive influence upon events, but it required Cordelia to spend herself in a holding action that drew the sting from evil and thereby made possible a traditionally defined order. Antony's power to become his flaw and yet to earn his reputation had no required effect upon the structure of order; but by its voluntariness it made an increment of value in the world, a new virtue independent of the continuing system of order. Prospero's submission, in abjuring magic and returning to Milan, combines the powers of Cordelia and Antony. It re-establishes order in Milan, but not by drawing evil to its own destruction, in the manner of Cordelia. Rather, in Alonso and Sebastian it transforms evil into renewed good by forgiveness. This renewal is achieved in Antony's manner, not by endurance, but by a voluntary surrender of utopia in exchange for the world. And it is a world still peopled by Caliban and Antonio, so that Prospero returned to Milan is a man who, having acknowledged the thing of darkness his, must still, like Antony, become his flaw. He must also submit himself anew to the endless possibility of disorder in the state.

Originally Prospero had neglected his public duty for his private pleasure. That, he told Miranda, made him vulnerable to the intrigues of Antonio, and eventually caused his exile from the kingdom. Then providence landed him safely on the island, leaving him free, unlike Antony, painlessly to choose the private life. But even without an equivalent of the opposed pressures of Octavius and Cleopatra to alert him to his need, Prospero voluntarily makes Antony's choice—despite the ever-threatened enmity of the world's Calibans and Antonios—of making his public and private interests conditional upon each other. That is of course the resolution appropriate to the genre of pastoral romance in which Shakespeare is working. But there is every reason to suppose that here as elsewhere Shakespeare employed his genre to suit his purpose. Prospero has enjoyed on his island all the security and comfort for which Lear yearned at the end. To exchange that now for the corrupt uses of the world, where, as Prospero says, "Every third thought shall be my grave," requires all the willingness to spend himself of which man is capable. But for Shakespeare at the end, nothing less will reconcile man to man and man to life. This magnanimity is the final step which transfigures man into the creator of his own brave world governed by its own benign providence.

The imagination of that world makes us capable of the amorality that I claimed at the beginning of this book is appropriate to *Antony and Cleopatra*—a vision in which friendship and enmity, like good and evil, are two sides of a coin, and therefore human brotherhood amidst human frailty is really possible. I think there is an episode in *Antony and Cleopatra* that goes far to capture the spirit of the play, when Dercetas brings the news of Antony's death to Caesar's camp:

Der.   He is dead, Caesar,
Not by a public minister of justice
Nor by a hired knife; but that self hand
Which writ his honour in the acts it did
Hath, with the courage which the heart did lend it,
Splitted the heart. This is his sword.
I robb'd his wound of it. Behold it stain'd
With his most noble blood.

Caes.   Look you sad, friends?
The gods rebuke me but it is tidings
To wash the eyes of kings!

Agr.   And strange it is
That nature must compel us to lament
Our most persisted deeds.

Maec.   His taints and honours
Wag'd equal with him.

Agr.   A rarer spirit never
— Did steer humanity; but you gods will give us
Some faults to make us men. Caesar is touch'd.

Maec. When such a spacious mirror's set before him,
He needs must see himself. (V.i.19–35)

Syntactically, rhythmically, and intellectually this is a single passage, as if written for the strings of a late Beethoven quartet.
Dercetas begins by explaining how Antony's suicide transcends
by its form of death Hamlet's dichotomy between minister and
scourge, and, by implication, Hamlet's corollary dichotomy
between to be and not to be: the stroke that split Antony's heart
also repaid its invaluable loan of courage and thereby made
the heart whole again. And then these worldly Romans make
a series of variations in each of which opposites are contained
and reconciled, culminating in Caesar and Antony as two sides
of a mirror. Here finally Rome's health is restored by the
magnanimity of Antony's suicide, which cements Caesar to
him by showing Caesar an image of himself in its mixture of
taints and honors that makes us men. In that restoration nobody
is permitted the separate peace of a bird cage or a magic cell,

but neither must we wonder whether it is better not to be. The play reveals us to ourselves so implicated in each other, with all our taints and vices, that our deepest identity and our greatest hope can only lie in the power of magnanimity, whether in the dare to single combat or in the gift of suicide. All we can do, the play tells us, is to spend ourselves freely toward each other; so doing, Antony and Cleopatra create those rare and perfect circumstances when suicide can make a man immortal.

Appendix

Shakespeare's Development and the

Dating of the Plays

THE DATING OF MANY SHAKESPEAREAN PLAYS IS SUFFICIENTLY uncertain that we cannot designate with confidence any particular sequence as the indestructible foundation for speculations concerning Shakespeare's development. This fact has led a number of scholars to remain skeptical of all but the most tentative and generalized descriptions of the playwright's development. We can be confident enough that *Romeo and Juliet* was written before *Antony and Cleopatra,* so this thinking goes, to justify an interest in the possible maturation reflected in Shakespeare's different treatment of the lovers in the two plays; but the uncertain chronological proximity of *Antony and Cleopatra* to *King Lear* effectively disqualifies our interest in a possible development involving these two plays. J. Leeds Barroll's recent article, "The Chronology of Shakespeare's Jacobean Plays and the Dating of *Anthony and Cleopatra,*" poses this problem with great lucidity, and presents a meticulously thorough examination both of the adequacy of traditional methods for dating the plays and of the relevant evidence available on the dating of *Antony and Cleopatra* in relation to other plays of this period. Although Barroll's scrupulous adjudication of the evidence does not lead him to upsetting new conclusions about the date of the play—he assigns the first performance to somewhere between February, 1605 and February, 1607—it does justify his claim for the sequence of these plays, that "we have no proof enabling us to deny such a hypothetical order as, e.g., *Othello, Antony, Coriolanus, Lear, Macbeth,* with *Pericles* and *Cymbeline* sandwiched in anywhere." In view of such possibilities, any effort to read Shakespeare's development through these Jacobean plays, especially one arguing for the relation between *King*

Lear and *Antony and Cleopatra* that I have claimed, might seem perilous. Barroll says,

> There would thus seem to be every reason to define that date for which one searches . . . as a date not of composition, but of performance, if only because such a quest at least poses a query that is theoretically answerable. Of course even this kind of date produces no biographical certainty in terms of artistic development. . . . But as an heuristic maneuver, the very search for a first performance may impose a discipline enabling us more successfully to evade the slips into aesthetic orderings to which any interested and intelligent student of Shakespeare is . . . bound to be prone.[1]

I should argue that the difficulties suggested here are more illusory than real, for two reasons. One is that the difference between "an heuristic maneuver" and "slips into aesthetic orderings" is mainly verbal. The only relevant date for truly ordering the plays is the date of composition; and to investigate instead the date of first performance, which unavoidably turns out to be a two-year range of possibilities from which no necessary inferences arise concerning the date of composition, is already to slip into an aesthetic preference for questions that are "theoretically answerable" even if in practice they are moot. The second and more important reason why this issue may be falsely posed is that among prolific artists, as in all of life, there is an unmistakable and saving difference between chronology and development. The ordering of the artifacts is necessarily linear, while the development of the artistry is normally zigzag, so that even if we were able to establish the dates of composition for Shakespeare's plays, we should hardly expect to propose any theory of his development wholly consistent with the actual order of the plays. In Shakespeare's plays or Rembrandt's paintings or Beethoven's music, our perception that artistic development does in fact occur is no less certain, and no more, than our conviction that *King Lear,* say, could not have been composed before 1599. But within each artist's development there are anticipations, digressions, "sports" and stagnations, which, no matter where they occur in the chronology, do not alter our proven awareness of the particular character and direction of the artistic development at hand. In Beethoven's development the *Eroica* symphony seems premature in relation to the whole chronology, while the last quartet, Op. 135, is altogether too late. In Rembrandt's development, the coherence of which has been remarkably demonstrated by Sir Kenneth Clark, it is evident that "The Conspiracy of Claudius Civilis" could not have come much earlier; but it is evident too that it need not have come at all. The magnificent remaining fragment of this work, which Clark calls "recklessly personal," demonstrably partakes of Rembrandt's development and of the influences to which it was subject; yet it lies outside the internal logic of that development. And of *Coriolanus* we know enough about its position in Shakespeare's chronology to embarrass all our efforts to fit it in his observable development between *Hamlet* and *The Tempest*.

Yet to deny the specific direction of Shakespeare's development on such grounds would be an abdication of judgment. To take another example, it is an accepted opinion that *King Lear* resolves with an air of finality several issues which it turns out are most urgently resumed in *Macbeth*. But everything psychologists tell us, as well as our experience of Shakespeare and of ourselves, makes it wholly credible that *Macbeth* should constitute a sort of corollary purgation to the resolution accomplished in *King Lear,* so that to our account of Shakespeare's development it is not decisive which play was written first. I think this distinction between chronology and development justifies my claim in this book that in Shakespeare's development *Antony and Cleopatra* goes beyond *King Lear,* just as Beethoven's next-to-last quartet, Op. 131, goes beyond his last. Even if Barroll's exhaustive analysis were to suggest, as in fact it does not, a new likelihood that *Antony and Cleopatra* precedes *King Lear* in the order of composition, I should insist upon the same justification for my aesthetic analysis of Shakespeare's development that he claims for historical analysis of Shakespeare's chronology. Of course the particular analysis I have offered must still be judged for itself. I claim here only the methodological as well as the aesthetic relevance of the enterprise.

Bibliographic Note

ANYBODY WHO WRITES ABOUT SHAKESPEARE MUST EXPERIENCE a variety of embarrassments. I am painfully aware how often I have had to go over familiar ground in my effort to buttress the general interpretation that I claim is new. At the same time I am aware how much Shakespearean criticism I have not read that might have taught me things I still need to know. On the other hand, in many parts of my analysis I cannot be sure where my own thinking begins and that which I have absorbed from others leaves off. Because of this fact, and because my whole analysis is largely interpretative, the footnotes that follow provide references only for my direct quotations and my major debts. For example, when I refer on page 96 in the text to the frequently observed *de contemptu* imagery in *Hamlet,* and in the note cite only a single article, it is not because I am ignorant of or indifferent to the important observations on this subject by A. C. Bradley, Lily B. Campbell, Wolfgang Clemen, T. S. Eliot, Harold Goddard, H. Granville-Barker, Ernest Jones, G. Wilson Knight, Caroline Spurgeon, D. A. Traversi, and several others; it is simply because Donald Howard's essay happened particularly to shape my understanding of this aspect of *Hamlet.*

I want to enumerate here some general debts to the critics and scholars whose work has informed my thinking, even if I have not taken occasion to allude to it in text or notes. The writings of Dr. Johnson and Coleridge have been part of my working equipment, along with A. C. Bradley, *Shakespearean Tragedy* (London, 1904); Geoffrey Bush, *Shakespeare and the*

Natural Condition (Cambridge, Mass., 1956); H. Granville-Barker, *Prefaces to Shakespeare* (Princeton, N.J., 1947); J. F. Danby, *Shakespeare's Doctrine of Nature* (London, 1951); T. S. Eliot, *Selected Essays, 1917–32* (New York, 1932); D. G. James, *The Dream of Learning* (Oxford, 1951); G. Wilson Knight, *The Wheel of Fire* (Oxford, 1930), and *The Imperial Theme* (Oxford, 1931); Arthur Sewell, *Character and Society in Shakespeare* (Oxford, 1951); Theodore Spencer, *Shakespeare and the Nature of Man* (Cambridge, Mass., 1942); Caroline F. E. Spurgeon, *Shakespeare's Imagery and What it Tells Us* (Cambridge, England, 1935); and E. M. W. Tillyard, *Shakespeare's History Plays* (London, 1951).

Beyond these pervasive debts, various aspects of my argument owe particular obligations to many other works. Both in agreement and disagreement, my treatment of *Antony and Cleopatra* is indebted to Sylvan Barnet, "Recognition and Reversal in *Antony and Cleopatra*," *SQ*, VII (1957), 331–34; J. Leeds Barroll, "The Chronology of Shakespeare's Jacobean Plays and the Dating of *Antony and Cleopatra*," in Gordon Ross Smith (ed.), *Essays on Shakespeare* (College Park, Pa., 1966); S. L. Bethell, *Shakespeare and the Popular Dramatic Tradition* (London, 1944); Lawrence E. Bowling, "Antony's Internal Disunity," *SEL*, IV (1964), 239–46; A. C. Bradley, *"Antony and Cleopatra,"* in his *Oxford Lectures on Poetry* (London, 1909); Maurice Charney, *Shakespeare's Roman Plays* (Cambridge, Mass., 1961); D. G. Cunningham, "Characterization of Shakespeare's Cleopatra," *SQ*, VI (1955), 9–17; J. F. Danby, *"Antony and Cleopatra,"* in his *Poets on Fortune's Hill* (London, 1952); Willard Farnham, *Shakespeare's Tragic Frontier* (Berkeley, 1950); Harold C. Goddard, *The Meaning of Shakespeare* (Chicago, 1951); L. C. Knights, "Shakespeare and Political Wisdom," *Sewanee Review,* LXI (1953), 43–55; M. W. MacCallum, *Shakespeare's Roman Plays and Their Background* (London, 1910); J. Middleton Murry, *Shakespeare* (New York, 1936); James E. Phillips, Jr., *The State in Shakespeare's Greek and Roman Plays* (New York, 1940); and Derek Traversi, *Shakespeare: The Roman Plays* (Stanford,

1963). Finally I want to mention the article by Dipak Nandy, "The Realism of *Antony and Cleopatra,*" in Arnold Kettle (ed.), *Shakespeare in a Changing World* (New York, 1964), pp. 172–94, which parallels my approach to the play, and which I did not see until my book was written.

My discussions of Shakespeare's history plays, *Julius Caesar, Hamlet, King Lear,* and *The Tempest* are indebted to the following works, in addition to many already cited: Kenneth Burke, "Antony in Behalf of the Play," in *The Philosophy of Literary Form* (Baton Rouge, 1941) ; J. V. Cunningham, *Woe or Wonder: The Emotional Effect of Shakespearean Tragedy* (Denver, 1951) ; Russel Fraser, *Shakespeare's Poetics* (London, 1962) ; Frank Kermode, "Introduction" to the new Arden edition of *The Tempest* (Cambridge, Mass., 1958) ; and Leonard Unger, "Deception and Self-Deception in Shakespeare's *Henry IV,*" in *The Man in the Name* (Minneapolis, 1956), pp. 3–17.

All citations of the plays are from *The Complete Works of Shakespeare,* ed. George Lyman Kittredge (Boston, 1936).

Notes

1. My analysis of Cleopatra's speech is inspired by S. L. Bethell, *Shakespeare and the Popular Dramatic Tradition* (London, 1944), especially pp. 39–41.

2. Geoffrey Bullough. *Narrative and Dramatic Sources of Shakespeare* (5 vols.; New York, 1957–64), V, 275.

3. Some representative readings of the play may be found in A. C. Bradley, *Oxford Lectures on Poetry* (London, 1909), pp. 279–310; Maurice Charney, *Shakespeare's Roman Plays* (Cambridge, Mass., 1961), pp. 79–141; John F. Danby, *Poets on Fortune's Hill* (London, 1952), pp. 128–52; Willard Farnham, *Shakespeare's Tragic Frontier* (Berkeley, Calif., 1950), pp. 139–205; M. W. MacCallum, *Shakespeare's Roman Plays and Their Background* (London, 1910), pp. 300–453; Brents Stirling, *Unity in Shakespearean Tragedy* (New York, 1956), pp. 157–92; D. A. Traversi, *Shakespeare: The Roman Plays* (Stanford, Calif., 1963), pp. 79–203; and Mark Van Doren, *Shakespeare* (New York, 1953), pp. 230–42.

4. On the general effect of this vein of imagery, see especially D. A. Traversi, *An Approach to Shakespeare* (London, 1938), pp. 116–27. But cf. Danby, *Poets on Fortune's Hill,* pp. 128–52.

5. Everybody who touches on this subject in indebted first of all to E. M. W. Tillyard, *The Elizabethan World Picture* (London, 1943) and *Shakespeare's History Plays* (London, 1951), as well as to Theodore Spencer, *Shakespeare and the Nature of Man* (Cambridge, Mass., 1942). The present book argues, if not directly with Tillyard and Spencer, then with the excessive influence of their work upon subsequent Shakespearean criticism. It argues also with an interpretation of the Roman plays that anticipates the work of Tillyard and Spencer: James E. Phillips, Jr., *The State in Shakespeare's Greek and Roman Plays* (New York, 1940).

6. Jacob Burckhardt, *The Civilization of the Renaissance in Italy* (New York, 1914), p. 129.

CHAPTER TWO

1. I borrow the term "Brobdingnagian imagery" from Bethell, *Shakespeare and the Popular Dramatic Tradition*, p. 117.

2. Bullough, *Narrative and Dramatic Sources of Shakespeare*, V, 283–85, 290–91.

3. *Ibid.*, V, 290.

4. Cf. Phillips, *The State in Shakespeare's Greek and Roman Plays*, pp. 186–90.

5. Harold C. Goddard, *The Meaning of Shakespeare* (Chicago, 1951), p. 572; cf. A. C. Bradley, *Oxford Lectures on Poetry*, pp. 288–89.

6. Bullough, *Narrative and Dramatic Sources of Shakespeare*, V, 292; 295–96.

CHAPTER THREE

1. Tillyard, *Shakespeare's History Plays*; A. O. Lovejoy, *The Great Chain of Being* (Cambridge, Mass., 1936). See also Lily B. Campbell, *Shakespeare's "Histories"* (San Marino, Calif., 1947).

2. T. S. Eliot, "Shakespeare and the Stoicism of Seneca," in *Selected Essays, 1917–1932* (New York, 1932), p. 111.

3. *Johnson on Shakespeare*, ed. Sir Walter Ralegh (London, 1908), p. 114.

4. Leonard Unger, "Deception and Self-Deception in Shakespeare's *Henry IV*," in *The Man in the Name* (Minneapolis, 1956), p. 17.

5. Tillyard, *Shakespeare's History Plays*, pp. 234–37.

6. Bullough, *Narrative and Dramatic Sources of Shakespeare*, IV, 397.

7. *Johnson on Shakespeare*, pp. 132–33.

8. Arthur Sewell, *Character and Society in Shakespeare* (Oxford, 1951), pp. 45–46.

9. Cf., for example, Phillips' discussion of the play in *The State in Shakespeare's Greek and Roman Plays*, pp. 172–205, with Bernard Breyer, "A New Look at *Julius Caesar*," in *Essays in Honor of Walter Clyde Curry* (Nashville, Tenn., 1954), pp. 161–81.

10. The concept of a "Caesar-idea" in the play was first suggested by G. Wilson Knight, "The Eroticism of *Julius Caesar*," in *The Imperial Theme* (London, 1931), pp. 25–35.

11. Most modern editors regard as textually indefensible both the duplicate revelation of Portia's death and the attribution to Brutus of the battlefield speech. See, e.g., J. Dover Wilson in the New Cambridge edition, *Julius Caesar* (Cambridge, 1949), pp. 179–80, 196–97, and T. S. Dorsch in the New Arden edition, *Julius Caesar* (Cambridge, Mass., 1955), pp. 106, 124. But it is clear from their explanations that both

NOTES

editors, like many others, resolve the textual *cruces* according to their already formulated interpretations of Brutus' character—a practice frequently resorted to by Dover Wilson despite his insistence that interpretation cannot begin until the text is established. The interpretation of Brutus' character offered here requires no marked tampering with the Folio text.

Chapter Four

1. My approach to *Hamlet* has been influenced particularly by Francis Fergusson, "*Hamlet, Prince of Denmark:* The Analogy of Action," in *The Idea of a Theater* (Princeton, N.J., 1949), pp. 98–142; Fredson Bowers, "Hamlet as Minister and Scourge," *PMLA,* LXX (September, 1955), 740–49, and "Dramatic Structure and Criticism: Plot in *Hamlet,*" *SQ,* XV, 2 (Spring, 1964), 207–18; Sister Miriam Joseph, "*Hamlet*: A Christian Tragedy," *SP,* LIX, 2 (April, 1962), 119–40; and above all by D. G. James, *The Dream of Learning* (Oxford, 1951), pp. 33–68.

2. James, *The Dream of Learning,* p. 42.

3. *Johnson on Shakespeare,* pp. 191–92; James, *The Dream of Learning,* p. 38; G. Wilson Knight, "An Essay on Life-Themes in *Hamlet,*" in *The Imperial Theme* (London, 1931), p. 101.

4. See, e.g., Donald R. Howard, "Hamlet and the Contempt of the World," *South Atlantic Quarterly,* LVIII (Spring, 1959), 167–75.

5. The phrase is from the title of John F. Danby's *Shakespeare's Doctrine of Nature: A Study of King Lear* (London, 1951), to which my analysis is deeply and variously indebted.

6. Here as in many parts of my analysis of *King Lear,* my thinking has been powerfully stimulated—the more so in disagreement—by many conversations with my former colleague Sigurd Burckhardt, and by his articles, "The King's Language: Shakespeare's Drama as Social Discovery," *Antioch Review,* XXI (Fall, 1961), 369–87, and "King Lear: The Quality of Nothing," *Minnesota Review,* I (Winter, 1961), 33–50.

7. See J. V. Cunningham, *Woe or Wonder: The Emotional Effect of Shakespearean Tragedy* (Denver, Colo., 1951), pp. 62–105.

8. John Holloway, *The Story of the Night* (London, 1961), p. 95.

9. The point was first made by A. C. Bradley, in *Shakespearean Tragedy* (London, 1904), pp. 256–60.

Chapter Five

1. John Middleton Murry, *Shakespeare* (New York, 1936), pp. 307–8.

Chapter Six

1. *Coleridge's Shakespearean Criticism,* ed. T. M. Raysor (2 vols.; Cambridge, Mass., 1930), I, 86.

2. Beyond its debt to Bethell and Wilson Knight, my analysis of this aspect of the play's style impinges upon those of Maurice Charney, *Shakespeare's Roman Plays,* pp. 79–93, and D. A. Traversi, *An Approach to Shakespeare,* pp. 115–27.

3. See Tillyard, *The Elizabethan World Picture,* pp. 81–93.

4. I borrow this resonant terminology from A. O. Lovejoy, *The Great Chain of Being.*

5. In *Shakespeare's Doctrine of Nature,* pp. 209 ff.

Postscript

1. My analysis of Caliban's role in variously indebted to Frank Kermode's Introduction to the New Arden edition of *The Tempest* (Cambridge, Mass., 1958), especially pp. xxxviii–xliii.

Appendix

1. Reprinted from an article by J. Leeds Barroll, "The Chronology of Shakespeare's Jacobean Plays and the Dating of *Anthony and Cleopatra,*" in *Essays on Shakespeare.* Published by the Pennsylvania State University Press, University Park, Pennsylvania, 1965. Pp. 121–22.

Index